"Among the most significant ch
in a world inundated with pride and arrogance is true humility. But what
is humility, and how does a Christian come to embody it? In *Growing
Downward: The Path of Christ-Exalting Humility*, Nick Thompson walks
through the biblical and redemptive-historical teaching about humility,
encouraging believers to understand what it is and how to possess it.
Rooting his teaching in biblical anthropology and Christology, Thompson helps us understand better the reasons we should pursue humility,
how Christ is the source and example of it, and how we can grow in it.
If you are looking to read a theologically rich and spiritually edifying
book, look no further."
—Nick Batzig, pastor of Church Creek PCA in Charleston,
South Carolina, and associate editor, Ligonier Ministries

"Christians can become lopsided, leaning toward how to think, live, or
feel better. Thompson's teaching on humility helps us view ourselves
more accurately and realistically, affecting every aspect of our lives. His
impressive breadth of application makes his teaching concrete rather
than abstract. This book establishes the right way of thinking and living
in light of who God is and who we are. What more could one want in
any book on theology or on Christian living?"
—Ryan M. McGraw, Morton H. Smith Professor of Systematic
Theology, Greenville Presbyterian Theological Seminary

"*Growing Downward* is the most robust, biblical, theological discussion of humility I've seen. Nick roots the discussion exactly where it
needs to begin—with a theology of God. He defines humility as 'the
downward disposition of a Godward self-perception.' Humility happens
when we see ourselves in light of the grandeur and grace of God. There
is nothing trite about this book. It is a mini theology, covering topics
from the character of God to the nature of sin, anthropology, Christology, soteriology, ecclesiology, and eschatology—all of it pointing to
the magnificent glory of God and the joy of true humility before Him.
The benefit of this book is that it doesn't merely talk about humility; it
actively helps readers *experience* humility as they are brought before the
truth of God. While the material is weighty, Nick uses personal illustra-
tions, stories, and notes that keep it moving along. But this is not a book

to be read quickly. The truths are too deep. It would make for a great small group Bible study. Highly recommended!"
—Dale VanDyke, senior pastor, Harvest Orthodox Presbyterian Church, Wyoming, Michigan

"In this much-needed, well-written, easy-to-read book on a critical subject for every Christian, Nick Thompson reminds us that real humility springs from knowing God and ourselves as both truly are. His book is a model of how theology should be applied to practical Christian living. He offers no manual on how to act humbly but provides biblical motivations to be humble. May God use this essential book in all of our lives so that we may genuinely confess with John the Baptist, '[Christ] must increase, and I must decrease.'"
—Joel R. Beeke, president, Puritan Reformed Theological Seminary, Grand Rapids, Michigan

"Defining *humility* as 'the downward disposition of a Godward, Christ-centered self-perception' in view of so much misconception, Thompson shows how relentlessly biblical the implications of this definition are for the life of the believer. Doctrinally penetrating, consistently pastoral, and highly readable, *Growing Downward* is as edifying as it is deeply searching."
—Richard B. Gaffin Jr., professor of biblical and systematic theology, emeritus, Westminster Theological Seminary

"When I was a child, my mother used to tell a fable about a man who won a medal for humility but had it taken away the moment he wore it. The point was obvious and has been proven by time: we are never as humble as we ought to be, nor even as humble as we wish to be. Yet by God's grace we can be humbler than we are right now, and it's for that reason that I recommend *Growing Downward*, a book that mines the Scriptures to show how to display a humility that is empowered by Christ and exalts the name of Christ."
—Tim Challies, blogger, author, and book reviewer

GROWING DOWNWARD

GROWING DOWNWARD

The Path of Christ-Exalting Humility

Nick Thompson

Reformation Heritage Books
Grand Rapids, Michigan

Growing Downward
© 2022 by Nick Thompson

Reformation Heritage Books
3070 29th St. SE
Grand Rapids, MI 49512
616-977-0889
orders@heritagebooks.org
www.heritagebooks.org

Unless otherwise indicated, Scripture taken from the New King James Version®. Copyright © 1982 by Thomas Nelson. Used by permission. All rights reserved.

Scripture quotations marked ESV are from The Holy Bible, English Standard Version® (ESV®), copyright © 2001 by Crossway, a publishing ministry of Good News Publishers. Used by permission. All rights reserved.

All italics in Scripture quotations have been added by the author.

Printed in the United States of America
22 23 24 25 26 27/10 9 8 7 6 5 4 3 2 1

Library of Congress Cataloging-in-Publication Data

Names: Thompson, Nick (Theologian), author.
Title: Growing downward : the path of Christ-exalting humility / Nick Thompson.
Description: Grand Rapids, Michigan : Reformation Heritage Books, [2022] | Includes bibliographical references.
Identifiers: LCCN 2021058092 (print) | LCCN 2021058093 (ebook) | ISBN 9781601789419 (paperback) | ISBN 9781601789426 (epub)
Subjects: LCSH: Humility—Religious aspects—Christianity. | BISAC: RELIGION / Christian Living / Spiritual Growth
Classification: LCC BV4647.H8 T46 2022 (print) | LCC BV4647.H8 (ebook) | DDC 241/.4—dc23/eng/20220121
LC record available at https://lccn.loc.gov/2021058092
LC ebook record available at https://lccn.loc.gov/2021058093

For additional Reformed literature, request a free book list from Reformation Heritage Books at the above regular or email address.

To Tessa,

*whose Christlike beauty captivates my
heart like none else here below*

Contents

Part 5: Eschatological Humility

Preface

"Pride is the number one enemy of the pastor at every stage of the game."

The statement echoed in my soul like a thunderous roar in a vacant corridor. These were not the words of a ministerial novice. They came from the lips of a man who had spent nearly four decades in the trenches of pastoral ministry.[1] I pondered his dogmatic assertion. *The number one enemy? At every stage of the game? Could this really be true?*

I had more than a sneaking suspicion that it was. The statement resonated with me. I had just graduated from seminary and was ready to change the world. I was eager to pour myself out in ordained pastoral ministry, fighting against evil in all of its forms. In these moments, however, God brought me face-to-face with my ultimate spiritual foe. And here was what was so alarming about it—this fiend lived within my chest.

Though I would have had a difficult time defining *pride* that day or explaining precisely how it was manifest in my life, I was sensible enough to recognize that I was proud. And I understood that if I didn't make war with it, my pride had the potential to debilitate, even destroy, my future ministry.

---

1. John Piper, "Advice to Young Pastors" (panel discussion #3, T4G, 2020), https://t4g.org/resources/ed-moore/advice-to-young-pastors/.

That summer was a wonderfully painful season as God gently peeled back layer after layer of pride within. He began to expose my natural bent toward self-promotion, self-protection, and self-pity. He enabled me to see how this infatuation with self bled into every facet of my existence, even into my service to Christ. By God's grace, I became persuaded that pride was indeed my number one enemy. What became equally clear as I studied the Scriptures, however, was that pride was deeply problematic not merely for pastors and those pursuing pastoral ministry but for every person on the face of the globe.

Your Greatest Foe

Here is the unvarnished truth: pride is *your* number one enemy at every stage of the game. This is true of you regardless of your vocation; your economic, political, or social status; and your age, ethnicity, or education. It is even true of you regardless of your spiritual condition, whether in Adam or in Christ. To be a human postfall is to be inundated with pride. And there is nothing that could possibly be more dangerous or harmful. Pride doesn't merely have the ability to destroy ministries; it has the ability to destroy men, women, boys, and girls. Left unchecked, it will obliterate you.

The focus of the book you are holding, however, is not the negative vice of pride, but the positive virtue of humility. So why begin in such a bleak, dismal manner? I begin here because it is only as we come to understand pride as our greatest enemy that we will learn to embrace humility as our greatest ally.

Your Chief Friend

If pride is our chief foe, then humility is our chief friend. All of us have acquaintances given to ear-tickling flattery. Humility is no such friend. It is a straight-shooting, tell-it-like-it-is, black-and-white kind of friend. Humility has no patience for unrealities. When it paints your portrait, you won't catch it smoothing over your pimples. Given our deeply ingrained arrogance, even the best among us find humility's company painful, sometimes even traumatic. We much prefer to surround ourselves with airbrushing flatterers.

All of us aspire to grow in prominence, power, and prosperity. Our tendency is to view life as an uphill climb. But spiritual growth is not an ascent; it is a descent. To grow in humility is to grow *downward*.[2] Quite frankly, that is not a pleasant experience. Why do you think so many kids want to be astronauts when they grow up, but no one wants to be a ditch digger or a coal miner? There is nothing impressive or exhilarating about getting down in the dirt. But that is precisely where humility is intent on taking us, and it is resolved to take us there because that is where we belong. Humility is concerned with reality, and the reality is that corrupt creatures like us are in our rightful place only when we are brought low with faces pressed to the dust before our Creator.

No Walk in the Park

Be warned: the pages ahead are aimed at bringing you low by God's grace. They were painful to write, and those who read them carefully and prayerfully will not come out unscathed. For years I have stayed in shape through a rigorous exercise program during which, as my body is about to collapse from exhaustion, the instructor has been known to bark, "The elite go past the point of comfort!" There is immense wisdom in that expression. God's elite are the humble, but the road to humility is no walk in the park. If we would grow as God wants us to, we must go past the point of comfort. You and I must crucify our inclinations toward fluffy, feel-good religion. Christianity is nothing of the sort. It is a call to die, for it is only as we die to ourselves that we can truly live.

By God's all-wise design, the painful path of humility is the one to true meaning and fulfillment. It is a path that can be trod only through union with Jesus Christ. He was the only truly humble

---

2. The phrase *growing downward* is taken from the nineteenth-century Anglican preacher Charles Simeon. See H. C. G. Moule, *Charles Simeon* (London: Inter-Varsity Fellowship, 1948), 64.

man ever to walk this earth, and He alone has the power to make us humble as He conforms us to His image by His indwelling Spirit. True humility can only ever be pursued in Him.

Would you join me in striving after humility by His power and for His glory? The path will not be easy, but I promise you that it will be worth it.

Toward a Definition of Humility

"You do not really understand something," quipped Albert Einstein, "unless you can explain it to your grandmother."

By nature, I am an intellectual. I enjoy reading and discussing theology at a deep level. I have a strange attraction to big ideas and big words. But one of the great blessings of being a father is that it keeps my feet tethered to planet earth. If I were to open family worship with an explanation of the etymological significance of the Greek word *perichoresis* as a segue into a twenty-minute lecture on the ontological Trinity, it would take an entire two seconds for my five-year-old's eyes to be glazed over with indifference. During my years as a seminary student, I came to realize that if I could not explain what I was learning in an understandable way to my children (or my grandmother), then I hadn't really learned.

Defining *humility* in a simple and clear way is no easy task. Some assert that the multifaceted complexity of this virtue defies a simple definition.[1] But is it possible that our inability to explain humility concisely and clearly has less to do with humility's intricacy and

---

1. For example, Christopher Hutchinson purposefully avoids giving a one-sentence definition of humility, declaring that the entirety of his two-hundred-plus-page book is his definition. *Rediscovering Humility: Why the Way Up Is Down* (Greensboro, N.C.: New Growth Press, 2018), 3. Though offering a minor critique here, I highly recommend Hutchinson's work, especially his treatment of humility in relation to the life of the local church.

more to do with our failure to understand it? In this introduction we will attempt to wrap our minds around the essential contours of this vital virtue.

Humility Defined by Activity

Humility is often explained in terms of what it does. In his classic work, Andrew Murray defines humility as "the place of entire dependence on God."[2] His definition concentrates on what humility does in relation to God. It completely relies on Him. If Murray's definition stresses the Godward activity of humility, then John Dickson's definition stresses the humanward activity of humility. According to Dickson, humility is "the noble choice to forgo your status, deploy your resources or use your influence for the good of others before yourself."[3] In other words, humility sacrificially spends itself for the sake of other people.

These are accurate and clear descriptions of what humility does. And there is certainly biblical warrant for describing humility in these ways (e.g., Phil. 2:3; James 4:6–7). But properly defining someone or something ordinarily requires moving beyond mere activity.

If you were to inquire about my wife, I could respond by saying, "Well, her skill in the kitchen is extraordinary. On top of that, she pours herself out in homeschooling our boys while still managing to keep the house clean and the laundry done. She is pretty great!" Anyone who knows Tessa knows all of that is wonderfully true. But if Tessa were to overhear my description of her, she would likely feel offended and undervalued. Why? Haven't I praised her? Sort of. I have praised her activity, not her person. Of course the two cannot be separated. It is the person who carries out the actions. But my

---

2. Andrew Murray, *Humility* (New Kensington, Pa.: Whitaker House, 1982), 16. J. Lanier Burns similarly defines *humility* as obedient and dependent submission to God. *Pride and Humility at War: A Biblical Perspective* (Phillipsburg, N.J.: P&R, 2018), 15, 24, 65.
3. John Dickson, Humilitas: *A Lost Key to Life, Love, and Leadership* (Grand Rapids: Zondervan, 2011), 24.

wife is far more than what she does. The large-hearted, godly woman she is explains her frenzy of loving service in the home.

Rather than defining people by what they do, we ought to define peoples' doings by who they are. Such is the case with humility. Is it true that humility depends on and submits to God? You better believe it. Does it lovingly serve others? Absolutely. But the more fundamental question we must ask is, *Why* does humility do these things? What is it about this virtue that makes it desperately cling to God and selflessly consider others? What is humility in its essence?

Humility Defined by Essence

To put it as concisely as I am able, humility is *the downward disposition of a Godward self-perception.* Admittedly, apart from further explanation this poetic mouthful has the potential to go over a person's head. But continue to read as we unpack the various contours of this definition together.

Humility Is a Downward Disposition

The word *humble* in both Hebrew and Greek is often translated "lowly," expressing the idea of being bowed down to the ground. The Scriptures draw a sharp contrast between "the humble" and "the haughty" (e.g., 2 Sam. 22:28; Pss. 18:27; 138:6). The lowliness of humility is not a physical, external attribute any more than haughtiness is. It is a disposition of the soul. That is why elsewhere God refers to the humble as those who are "lowly in spirit."

> One's pride will bring him low,
>   but he who is *lowly in spirit* will obtain honor.
> (Prov. 29:23 ESV)

> For thus says the One who is high and lifted up,
>   who inhabits eternity, whose name is Holy:
> "I dwell in the high and holy place,
>   and also with him who is of a contrite and *lowly spirit*,
> to revive *the spirit of the lowly*,
>   and to revive the heart of the contrite. (Isa. 57:15 ESV)

Here is the essence of humility—lowliness of spirit.

From beginning to end, Christianity is concerned with the heart. Likely drawing from Old Testament texts like Proverbs 4:23, Jesus taught that every action and word of a person proceeds from the heart (Matt. 15:19). This is of central significance—before humility ever acts, it is first an internal frame of the soul.[4] And this inner constitution is directed downward. The spirit of the humble is not lifted up with self-conceit.

This is in contrast with pride. Pride manifests itself in a self-sufficient rejection of God and an abuse of others for selfish gain. But like humility, pride must be defined by its essence, not its activity. If humility is a downward disposition, then pride is a haughty disposition. In the great Old Testament text on humility, Proverbs 3:34, Solomon classifies the proud as "the scornful" (elsewhere translated "the scoffers"): "Surely He scorns the scornful, but gives grace to the humble." He later provides a concise explanation of the scorner as a "proud and haughty man…[who] acts with arrogant pride" (21:24). Solomon heaps word upon word to explain the egotistical, high-minded arrogance of the scoffer, and that makes a lot of sense when you think about the nature of scoffing. How can people perpetually mock God or others? Only after they have elevated themselves to the position of judge. Interestingly, one of the chief character traits of scoffers is that they cannot stand to be rebuked by others (e.g., 13:1; 15:12). They have deceived themselves into believing they are beyond criticism or correction. They are the epitome of those who possess a high-minded, haughty spirit.

---

4. We typically speak of three faculties comprising the human soul—the mind, the will, and the affections. Humility has its seat in the affections. I am, therefore, using the term *disposition* synonymously with *affection*. But by affection, I do not mean a flash-in-the-pan feeling or mindless emotion; I mean an intense inclination of heart that is informed by truth (the mind) and leads to action (the will). Humility is an intense inclination downward. To read further on the nature of holy affections, see Gerald R. McDermott, *Seeing God: Jonathan Edwards and Spiritual Discernment* (Vancouver: Regent College Publishing, 1995), 27–41.

We see, therefore, that humility is a downward disposition of soul in contrast to pride, which unduly exalts the self. But to stop with the definition there is to leave the door open to potential confusion. Not every lowly disposition is humble. Modern psychology has popularized a form of lowliness lacking in humility. It is called low self-esteem. If you don't personally struggle with low self-esteem, you likely know someone who does. Such a person lacks confidence, being perpetually plagued with feelings of inferiority, incompetency, and hypersensitivity. It is easy to confuse low self-esteem with humility. But this lack of self-confidence, while having many potential secondary causes, has a singular primary cause. It is only because the soul has raised the self to the level of highest importance that it can be so distraught over its inherent weaknesses, failures, and oppression.[5] People with low self-esteem are no less consumed with themselves than people with high self-esteem. This kind of lowly spirit is simply a veiled form of pride. Low self-esteem is a haughty spirit clothed in the garments of a false humility.

It will not do, then, for us to merely say that humility is a downward disposition of soul, for not all downward dispositions are created equal.

Humility Is Produced by a Godward Self-Perception
Humility is a certain kind of lowly spirit. It is brought about by seeing ourselves in the light of God's glory. This is what I call *a Godward self-perception*.

---

5. Low self-esteem is complex and does have varied secondary causes or triggers. For example, a child may lack confidence because of his father's verbal abuse ("Dad is right; I am good-for-nothing."), or a wife may struggle with the same due to a husband's pornography addiction ("If only I were as attractive as those women, then my husband would love me."). These are tragic realities that cannot be quickly dismissed or ignored. But they are nonetheless secondary causes of low self-esteem. The primary cause is always an unhealthy fixation on the self.

William Farley defines humility as "the capacity to see myself in God's light."[6] This definition is on to something vital about humility, though it actually misses the essence of humility. Humility is not the ability or capacity to have a Godward self-perception. It is the downward disposition that is brought about by such a God-entranced vision of the self. It is the internal frame of the soul that results from seeing ourselves before the face of God. It is not the power of sight, but the product of sight.

This is why humility is intimately related to the fear of the Lord in the Scriptures. For example, Proverbs 15:33 states, "The fear of the LORD is the instruction of wisdom, and before honor is humility." By way of synonymous parallelism, Solomon draws a close connection between these two virtues. Again, he writes, "By humility and the fear of the LORD are riches and honor and life" (22:4). The fear of God is not entirely synonymous with humility. They are distinct graces. But the downward disposition of biblical humility is always wed to the fear of God. The two can never be separated.

John Murray defines the fear of God as "the controlling sense of the majesty and holiness of God and the profound reverence which this apprehension elicits." It is "the reflex in our consciousness of the transcendent majesty and holiness of God."[7] The fear of God is reflexive. It is a disposition of loving reverence necessarily evoked by beholding the living God.[8]

---

6. William Farley, *Gospel-Powered Humility* (Phillipsburg, N.J.: P&R, 2011), 24. Later he defines it as "the God-given ability to see self and God as we really are" (37).

7. John Murray, *Principles of Conduct: Aspects of Biblical Ethics* (Grand Rapids: Eerdmans, 1957), 236–37. Elsewhere Murray writes, "The fear of God means that God is constantly in the centre of our thought and apprehension, and life is characterized by the all-pervasive consciousness of dependence upon him and responsibility to him." *The Epistle to the Romans* (Grand Rapids: Eerdmans, 1959), 1:105.

8. In the Scriptures, loving God and fearing God are largely synonymous realities (e.g., Ps. 145:19–20). Michael Reeves explains that "the trembling 'fear of God' is a way of speaking about the intensity of the saints' love for and enjoyment of all that God is.... True fear of God is true love for God defined: it is

Wherever you find this profound reverence drawn from the controlling consciousness of God's glory, there will of necessity be humility. Given Murray's definition of the fear of God, we could define humility as *the profound lowliness elicited by the controlling sense of our own creatureliness and corruption.* As we are gripped by the majesty of God, we come to see ourselves as finite, dependent creatures. As we behold the holiness of God, we come to see ourselves as radically corrupt sinners, and this perception produces a downward disposition of soul. As the soul grows upward in the fear of God, it grows downward in humility.[9]

If you happen to be a multimillionaire who lives in Dubai, you might consider renting a luxurious apartment at the Burj Khalifa. At the time of writing, this skyscraper is the tallest building in the world, reaching 2,716 feet into the air. For a building to stand that tall requires a foundation that reaches deep into the ground. The foundation of the Burj Khalifa plumbs 164 feet below the earth and is made of 110,000 tons of concrete and steel. That is how the fear of God and humility work. To grow upward in fear requires growing downward in humility, and vice versa. The higher up we grow in knowing God, the lower down we must grow in knowing ourselves.

Redemptive history is filled with graphic pictures of this interplay between humility and the fear of God. One such picture is the righteous man Job. In the face of traumatic suffering and less-than-helpful friends, Job questioned the wisdom of God's rule. He wanted an explanation for the sudden agonizing and seemingly random loss of his riches, family, and health. And finally, at the end of the book,

---

the right response to God's full-orbed revelation of himself in all his grace and glory." *Rejoice and Tremble: The Surprising Good News of the Fear of the Lord* (Wheaton, Ill.: Crossway, 2021), 52–53. So when speaking of the fear of God, I understand such affectionate reverence to fulfill the first and greatest commandment: "You shall love the LORD your God with all your heart, with all your soul, and with all your mind" (Matt. 22:37).

9. My language here is indebted to John Piper's description of the spirituality of Charles Simeon as "growing downward in humility and growing upward in adoring communion with God." *21 Servants of Sovereign Joy: Faithful, Flawed, and Fruitful* (Wheaton, Ill.: Crossway, 2018), 320.

God explains Himself. He appears in a whirlwind of glory, asking Job seventy-seven questions, beginning with this one: "Where were you when I laid the foundations of the earth?" (Job 38:4). This barrage of divine questions was intended to drive home a singular point: "Job, I am God, and you are not." Such was not the explanation Job was looking for, but it was the one he most needed. Job's encounter with the uncreated majesty of God left him crying out,

> I have heard of You by the hearing of the ear,
>> But now my eye sees You.
> Therefore I abhor myself,
>> And repent in dust and ashes. (42:5–6)

Don't miss the "therefore." It introduces the reflexive result of Job's vision of God. The reflex of his fear of the Lord was humility. Job, beholding the perfections of God, was laid in the dust. The upward gaze of fear led to the downward disposition of humility.

The great problem with the proud is that they have willfully forgotten God. Pride, writes C. S. Lewis, is "the complete anti-God state of mind."[10] Arrogant people deify the self. Their haughty disposition is elicited from the controlling sense of their own supposed greatness and impeccability. They haven't learned to see themselves before the face of God. In the words of the psalmist, "There is no fear of God before his eyes" (Ps. 36:1).

No wonder John Calvin began his *Institutes* by telling us that "man is never sufficiently touched and affected by the awareness of his lowly state until he has compared himself with God's majesty."[11] If we would have a disposition of soul that accords with how lowly we truly are by nature, we must see ourselves before God. We must have a Godward self-perception.

Such a notion, however, calls into question that humility consists in forgetting about the self, an idea popularized by Tim Keller in *The Freedom of Self-Forgetfulness*. As he makes clear from the title, Keller

---

10. C. S. Lewis, *Mere Christianity* (New York: HarperCollins, 2001), 122.
11. John Calvin, *Institutes of the Christian Religion*, trans. Ford Lewis Battles, ed. John T. McNeill (Philadelphia: Westminster Press, 1960), 1.1.3.

defines humility as "thinking of myself less." He explains, "The truly gospel-humble person is a self-forgetful person."[12] Keller's application of the gospel to both high and low self-esteem is immensely insightful. His description of a "gospel-humble person" as someone who has been freed through Christ from a love affair with self is likewise biblical.

My concern is over the language of *forgetting* and *not thinking*.[13] The Bible never calls us to banish the self from our thoughts. Keller focuses on the teaching of Paul to derive his definition of humility, but nowhere does Paul discourage us from thinking about the self. In fact, possibly more than any other biblical writer, Paul is intent on impressing on us who we are, either in Adam or in Christ. The apostle actually desires you to think about yourself, but he desires you to think about yourself *rightly* before the face of the triune God of creation and redemption. Much of Keller's book is about how the gospel, particularly justification by faith, leads to self-forgetting freedom.[14] But in order to understand my righteous status in Christ so that it is working itself out in others-oriented love, I need to remember, not forget, myself. Humility is not produced by losing sight of our self but by properly perceiving our self as we relate to God and others.

So there are two dominant movements of the soul here. The soul grows upward in fear toward God and downward in humility toward self. And the upward grace of fear together with the downward grace of humility leads us to grow in the outward grace of love.

Humility Is Productive of Love toward Others

Again, Job provides us with a striking picture of this. Job's friends had genuinely tried to comfort him. They had the best of intentions.

---

12. Timothy Keller, *The Freedom of Self-Forgetfulness: The Path to True Christian Joy* (Leyland, Lancashire, UK: 10Publishing, 2012), 32–33.

13. Lewis also wields the concept of self-forgetfulness favorably: "The real test of being in the presence of God is that you either forget about yourself altogether or see yourself as a small, dirty object. It is better to forget about yourself altogether." *Mere Christianity*, 125.

14. Keller, *Freedom of Self-Forgetfulness*, 37–44.

But unfortunately good intentions don't always lead to good results. They were terrible counselors with a truncated view of God. Job was rightly frustrated with them for their false accusations and vicious critique. We wouldn't be surprised to find him yelling, "Sayonara!" and ditching such rotten company. But after God presses Job's face to the dirt before His greatness, He turns to rebuke Job's three friends. They had sinfully misrepresented God in their thoughts and words. They needed a priest to intercede on their behalf, and God provides such an intercessor through righteous Job (Job 42:7–8). Remarkably, Job prays for these men as the blood of animals is spilled for their sin (vv. 8–9). His friends who had betrayed him in his time of greatest need become the objects of his loving intercession. How could that happen? Surely Job's natural response was to say, "It's called karma. You poured forth wrath on me, and now you are getting what you deserve!" But instead, Job offers up prayers for his enemies. Job's love was a work of grace resulting from the lowly spirit elicited through his encounter with God.

The downward disposition of a Godward self-perception frees us to love other people selflessly and sacrificially. This is why humility is often connected with loving others (e.g., Eph. 4:2; Phil. 2:3; 1 Peter 3:8). It is also why the fear of the Lord is often connected with keeping God's commands summarized by love (e.g., Ps. 19:9; Eccl. 12:13).

This diagram illustrates the relationship between humility, God-fear, and love. Here is what we must see: the profound low-liness of humility together with the profound reverence of fear liberate us to love profoundly.

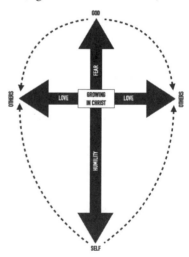

A Definition of Humility

These three movements of upward fear, downward humility, and outward love naturally give rise to three questions:

1. How do I view God? (i.e., Do I fear Him?)
2. How do I view myself? (i.e., Am I lowly in spirit?)
3. How do I view others? (i.e., Do I love other people tangibly and from the heart?)

If you quickly skimmed over these questions, please go back and prayerfully ponder them. They are instruments by which you can gauge your humility, but probably not in the way you first imagined. Humility is not measured by the level of piety exemplified in your answers, but by the level of pain inflicting your heart as you answer. Those who are inundated with pride will possess a blind indifference toward their haughtiness, often clothing it in pious religiosity. Just think of how a first-century Pharisee might have answered these questions. It is only when we are truly humble that we see how lacking in humility we truly are. As paradoxical as it is, those who possess a lowly spirit are those who lament their lack of such a God-fearing, people-loving, downward disposition of soul. What do your answers reveal about your heart?

This introduction has been a mere pencil sketch of humility's portrait. There is great need for this preliminary drawing to be filled in with living color, and so the chapters that follow could be likened to distinct paint colors applied to the canvas. The book's five parts attempt to grapple with diverse, God-centered perspectives on the self.

Growing Downward is an elementary primer on a Godward self-perception. But only the Spirit of Christ can take these God-saturated truths about the self and drive them home to your heart in such a way that you actually grow downward. As you read on, plead with Him to do this gracious work. God forbid that we would rest content growing in the understanding of humility without growing in humility itself.

PART 1

Existential Humility

existential: pertaining to existence or being
We are dependent, covenantal, and temporal creatures.

◆ CHAPTER 1 ◆

Dependent Creatures

Have you ever experienced the frustration of walking into a movie twenty minutes after the opening credits? The protagonist and antagonist have already been introduced. The plot has begun to unfold, and the suspense is building. As a result of missing the initial scenes, you spend the next hour and a half annoyed, trying to figure out what in the world is going on.

Beginnings are important. They set the stage and provide an essential framework of understanding. And this is no less true when it comes to humility. Unfortunately, in our theologizing about humility, we often show up twenty minutes late.

The Beginning of Humility

When did humility first arrive on the scene? The common assumption is that this virtue made its initial appearance after the fall into sin. One author defines humility as "honestly assessing ourselves in light of God's holiness and our sinfulness."[1] Another describes it similarly as "the capacity to see myself in God's light, in the context of his holiness and my sinfulness."[2] These statements are generally true as far as they go. For people like us living after the fall,

---

1. C. J. Mahaney, *Humility: True Greatness* (Colorado Springs: Multnomah, 2005), 22.
2. Farley, *Gospel-Powered Humility*, 24.

humility's downward disposition is produced in part by perceiving our sinfulness before God's transcendent purity. The problem is that these definitions ground humility's essence in man's fall. Humility, according to these definitions, requires sinfulness. But knowledge of sinfulness is actually not essential to humility, nor is the fall into sin the beginning of humility.

This becomes plain when we consider the quintessential humble man, Jesus Christ. Our Savior possessed no ability to assess Himself as sinful before God's holiness because He was without sin (2 Cor. 5:21; Heb. 4:15). If we root humility in the fall and make knowledge of personal sinfulness essential to its nature, then we must conclude that the incarnate Son of God was not humble. But the Scriptures emphatically tell us otherwise (Matt. 11:29; Phil. 2:5–8). Along with this, the root of the first sin in the garden was pride. We cannot make sense of the arrogant rebellion that caused humankind's fall, however, unless there was a prior disposition of humility. Humility did not arrive on the scene at the fall. Rather, it was viciously assaulted at the fall, and such an assault presupposes its former presence.

Humility's debut was not the fall of man, but the creation of man. In our thinking about humility, we must begin at the very beginning.

Independent Creator, Dependent Creatures

The Bible opens with the words, "In the beginning God" (Gen. 1:1). As the eternally uncreated One, God has always existed. He simply is, and He depends on nothing and no one to be who He is. In theology, we call this God's *aseity*, a term derived from the Latin phrase *a se*. Literally, it means "of himself" or "from himself."

Aseity encompasses a number of truths about the being of God. First, God is self-existent. He has life of Himself, independent of all that is outside of Him. Second, God is self-sufficient. He does not depend on anything or anyone to continue to be who He is or to carry out His sovereign purposes. Third, God is self-satisfied. He relies on nothing in creation to be fulfilled or content.

This was Paul's message at the Areopagus. Standing in the midst of these Athenians and their pantheon of man-made gods (idols dependent on the humans who formed them), the apostle proclaimed God's aseity: "God, who made the world and everything in it, since He is Lord of heaven and earth, does not dwell in temples made with hands. Nor is he worshiped with men's hands, as though He needed anything, since He gives to all life, breath, and all things" (Acts 17:24–25). Our God needs absolutely no one and nothing to be who He is. He doesn't need you. He doesn't need me. He exists eternally in triune divine fullness. Notice how Westminster Confession 2.2 puts it: "God hath all life, glory, goodness, blessedness, in and of himself; and is alone in and unto himself all-sufficient, not standing in need of any creatures which he hath made, nor deriving any glory from them, but only manifesting his own glory, in, by, unto, and upon them." God is independent in an absolute sense. He is *a se*.

At first glance, this might appear to be a theological rabbit trail. Aren't we talking about humility? What does a fancy Latin term touting God's independence have to do with your humility and mine? Actually, it has everything to do with it! Humility, you will recall, is the downward disposition of a *Godward* self-perception. The Bible sets our creation within the wider context of God's uncreated glory.

The Hebrew word for *create* only ever has God as the subject.[3] The sole uncreated One is the sole Creator. While we are called to fill, subdue, rule, and order creation, you and I are never cocreators with God. We are not creators; we are creatures. Three times this is stressed in Genesis 1:27: "So *God created* man in His own image; in the image of God *He created* him; male and female *He created* them." Man is uniquely created to reflect and represent the likeness of his Maker. To be God's image bearers is the height of creaturely dignity and privilege. It is our creation in the image of God that provides an initial window into the nature of humility. "The incipient beginning of humility's antithesis to pride," writes J. Lanier Burns,

---

3. Bruce K. Waltke with Cathi J. Fredricks, *Genesis: A Commentary* (Grand Rapids: Zondervan, 2001), 59.

"is rooted in God's creation of humanity in his image."[4] And that is because to be image involves unqualified dependence on the independent Original.

Our Dependence for Existence and Sustenance

My ten-month-old son, Vos, loves looking at his reflection in the mirror. A mirror is a piece of metal-layered glass. Its purpose is to reflect whatever stands in front of it. Vos loves the mirror not because he has a particular fondness of aluminum, but because he is fond of looking at himself. And who could fault him? He is a handsome little chap. (I've been told he looks a lot like his dad.) But to keep our boy from vanity, we don't allow him to spend his days admiring his good looks in the bathroom mirror. When my wife or I pick him up and take him into another room, do you know what happens to his image in the mirror? It vanishes. Vos's image simply cannot exist apart from Vos himself. The image is entirely dependent on the original.

That is precisely how it is with us as image of God. We are entirely dependent on the One whom we image. And it is this unqualified dependence that fundamentally sets us apart from our Creator. Only God, declares Anselm, "has of himself all that he has, while other things have nothing of themselves. And other things, having nothing of themselves, have their only reality from him."[5] While God is self-existent, we depend entirely on God for our existence. While God is self-sufficient, we depend entirely on God for our sustenance. Our Creator is the one who "gives to all life, breath, and all things" (Acts 17:25). To be a creature means that we derive our existence and our sustenance from Him.

When we come to possess a controlling sense of our creatureliness, it will elicit the profound lowliness of humility. The humble recognize that they are radically and entirely dependent on God

---

4. Burns, *Pride and Humility at War*, 21.
5. Anselm of Canterbury, *On the Fall of the Devil*, in *The Major Works*, ed. Brian Davies and G. R. Evans (Oxford: Oxford University Press, 1998), 1:194.

for life and breath. They know "that God is the source of all things, the means of all things, and the goal of all things."[6] Everything—absolutely everything—we are and have is from God and for His glory.

If you are a Bible-believing Christian, you will doubtless affirm these truths. But it is one thing to have God's uncreated independence and our image-bearing dependence neatly filed away in the mind and another thing entirely to embrace them with the heart.

I drive a 2016 Hyundai Sonata. It has cloth seats and a decent-sized dent on the front bumper. It is nothing fancy, but it is reliable, clean, and relatively charming. Recently while driving on the highway, I began to notice myself doing something strange. As I passed by people driving older and less desirable cars, a subtle sense of superiority would rise up within my heart. That's right, I was esteeming myself as more valuable than those around me because the piece of metal I was sitting in was a 2016 instead of a 1987! What could possibly cause me to reason in such a bizarre manner? It was, among other things, an unconscious denial of my creatureliness. I was operating under the assumption that my Hyundai, the money that enabled me to purchase it, the vocation that enabled me to earn the money, and the health and talents that enabled me to fulfill the vocation were not given to me by my Creator but were intrinsic to me. Sad to say, this was not a random, once-in-a-lifetime occurrence. I do this all the time. The girl sitting across the coffee shop from me is less of a person because she is working on an old HP while I type away on a new MacBook. The cashier at the drive-through window possesses less value than I do because she presumably doesn't have a graduate degree. The guy at the gym is beneath me because I can bench press more than he can. (Okay, I never actually struggle with this one!) Where do these haughty thoughts come from? They proceed from a failure to reckon with the fact that my life, my breath, and my everything is from another. "Who makes you differ from

---

6. Wayne A. Mack, *Humility: The Forgotten Virtue* (Phillipsburg, N.J.: P&R, 2005), 29.

another? And what do you have that you did not receive? Now if you did indeed receive it, why do you boast as if you had not received it?" (1 Cor. 4:7).

As creatures we have nothing that is not from God. As image we are entirely dependent on the Original for our existence, our sustenance, our abilities, our relationships, and our possessions. Absolutely everything we have has been received from God! Therefore, it is the height of insanity to boast in self. The only reasonable response to such all-encompassing dependence is the downward disposition of humility. Apart from God we are and have nothing.

Our Dependence for Identity and Purpose

Our age, possibly more than any previous one, is obsessed with personal identity. A few months ago, I took one of my boys to a doctor's appointment. As we waited in the exam room, a poster caught my attention. It had a colorful picture of what looked like a gingerbread man. The title, however, informed me that this "cookie" was not a gingerbread man but "The Genderbread Person." On the wall of an otherwise harmless doctor's office was a poster seeking to help my elementary-aged son determine his gender identity and sexual orientation! Here is a portion of what it said: "Gender identity is how *you*, in *your* head, think about *yourself*. It's the chemistry that composes *you* (e.g., hormonal levels) and how *you* interpret what that means" (emphasis mine). That is not an exaggerated paraphrase; those were the exact words.

Here is the message culture is drilling into our heads from the youngest conceivable age—your identity is whatever you think or feel yourself to be. You are the interpreter of yourself. You are the definer of you.

To be image of God, however, means that we don't get to define ourselves. Let's return to little Vos sitting in front of the bathroom mirror. When he smiles, what will happen to his image in the mirror? It will reflect the same toothy grin. When his older brother pinches him and makes him cry, what will be the resulting image in the mirror? It will be a distressing wail. Here is the point. The image is defined by the original. Vos's image cannot decide to grow a beard and start playing the ukulele unless that is what Vos himself is actually doing. The image doesn't get to call the shots. It is not free to be whoever or do whatever it pleases.

Such is the case with God's image. At creation God did not leave it to Adam and Eve to define themselves. As their Creator, He authoritatively declared, "Let Us make man in Our image, according to Our likeness" (Gen. 1:26). God sovereignly determined their identity. He did not say, "Adam, why don't you perform some yoga along with these Middle Eastern breathing techniques, and as you do, look deep within yourself to discover your true meaning and purpose." As Creator, He authoritatively declared, "Be fruitful and multiply; fill the earth and subdue it; have dominion" (v. 28). God sovereignly determined their purpose. The grand assumption of Genesis 1 is that at every point man is under the sovereign Creator, entirely dependent on Him for definition. Is that not what we would expect of an image? God alone as the independent Original is self-defined.

Our culture is fraught with identity confusion—even chaos—for the simple reason that it has banished God from its consideration. Contrary to popular thought, we do not find ourselves by looking inside of ourselves but by looking outside of ourselves to our Creator. To be image implies that we are defined by the Original. The downward disposition of humility reckons with this. Those who possess a lowly spirit bow before God's word as the only reliable interpretation of who they are.

But here is the problem: in our pride we don't want to be dependent images. Our inbred arrogance looks to anything but God for a sense of self. We look within. We look to other people. We look to money or beauty or talent. In other words, we are idolatrous. Pride is always looking to the creature for dignity and meaning rather than the Creator. This is what happens when I puff myself up with self-importance, thinking I'm pretty great because of my car or laptop or education. I am rooting my identity in created things. It is pride.

What may be harder to recognize, however, is that self-degrading thoughts are equally rooted in an idolatrous identity. Perhaps, like me, your lack of biceps tempts you to feel inferior. Or maybe you beat yourself up over your poor social skills or your less-than-luxurious home or your unimpressive résumé. Any number of things in our lives may tempt us to feel insecure and insignificant, but do you know the source of them all? It is a lack of a *Godward* self-perception. The reason you are ashamed to tell your neighbor that you work as a third-shift janitor is because you allow your job to define you. The reason your singleness is devastating is because you measure your worth by the lack of a spouse at your side. Low self-esteem is fueled by the same idolatrous pride as high self-esteem. Both seek to define the self in terms of the created rather than the Creator. Whether a boyfriend or bank account, brains or biceps, to the extent that you draw your identity from anything created, you are succumbing to pride. You are denying your image-bearing dependence on the God you were created to reflect.

Our Dependence for Satisfaction

Our Creator is a relational being. He is triune. The three persons of the Trinity—Father, Son, and Holy Spirit—have existed in the most incomprehensibly sweet communion from all eternity. Observe how Jonathan Edwards puts it: "God is infinitely happy in the enjoyment of himself, in perfectly beholding and infinitely loving, and rejoicing in, his own essence and perfections."[7] In other words, God is self-satisfied. He didn't create us because He was lonely or because there was some gaping hole in His being that needed to be filled. He is *a se.*

God's creation of the world was the overflow of His infinite, joyous fullness. He created you and me uniquely as His image in order to summon us into the orbit of His loving enjoyment and rejoicing. Geerhardus Vos is surely correct when he asserts that the image of

---

7. Jonathan Edwards, *Discourse on the Trinity*, in *The Works of Jonathan Edwards*, vol. 21, *Writings on the Trinity, Grace, and Faith*, ed. Sang Hyun Lee (New Haven, Conn.: Yale University Press, 2003), 113.

God "means above all that [man] is disposed for communion with God."[8] Image entails communion with the original. This is no cold, formalistic fellowship. Man and woman, as image, were created in a filial bond of devotion to God as their Father. When Adam was fruitful and multiplied, the result was a son born in Adam's image. Moses explains that Adam "begot a son in his own likeness, after his image, and named him Seth" (Gen. 5:3). Like father, like son. "To be a son," argues Sinclair Ferguson, "and to be the image and likeness of your father, are synonymous ideas."[9] This provides us with a window into the nature of the communion the image was intended to have with God. Adam, as son of God (Luke 3:38), was to bask in his Father's love and reciprocate that love. Unlike every other creature, humankind was not to relate to God as *mere* Creator but as *fatherly* Creator. Image bearers are "disposed for [filial] communion with God."

The appearance of my little boy's image in the mirror implies that the original is close at hand. Apart from his nearness, there could be no image. This fundamental connection between the image and the original falls just short of communion. Since Vos's image in the mirror is impersonal, there can be no genuine, living fellowship between it and the original. While Vos might delight in the image as it accurately reflects him, the image has no ability to reciprocate that delight in Vos. Communion is simply impossible without two personal beings.[10] We, however, are personal beings, created to live near our personal, fatherly Creator in loving fellowship. This gets to the heart of what it means to be image of God.

---

8. Geerhardus Vos, *Reformed Dogmatics*, vol. 2, *Anthropology*, trans. and ed. Richard B. Gaffin Jr. (Bellingham, Wash.: Lexham, 2012), 13.

9. Sinclair B. Ferguson, *Children of the Living God: Delighting in the Father's Love* (Edinburgh: Banner of Truth, 1989), 6–7.

10. John Owen describes communion as a "mutual communication in giving and receiving." *Communion with God*, in *The Works of John Owen*, ed. William H. Goold (Edinburgh: Banner of Truth, 1965), 2:9. This is a helpful definition, highlighting that fellowship is possible only between two distinct, personal beings. An impersonal object cannot participate in active communication with another by way of giving and receiving.

A closer look at the creation account within the context of covenant history reveals that the garden of Eden was no ordinary garden. It was a temple, the house of God. Adam was placed within it as a priestly son of God, commissioned to tend to this garden-temple, guard it from unholy intrusion, and extend its borders to the ends of the earth.[11] Humankind was created to live with God. The image was made for relationship with the Original.

It is for this reason that our re-creation in the image of God is spoken of in terms of knowledge. Paul refers to Christians as those who "have put on the new man who is renewed in knowledge according to the image of Him who created him" (Col. 3:10). This Spirit-wrought renewal is "a change to a previous, preferable state."[12] Man was originally created as God's image in knowledge. He was designed not merely to have an intellectual knowledge about God but to know God spiritually.[13] Tragically, he willfully forfeited that knowledge through sin. Through union with Christ, however, the capacity to know God as Father—to delight in Him through a loving communion bond—is progressively restored. To be God's image is to be disposed to knowing God as our chief joy and treasure.

While God is infinitely satisfied in Himself, we depend entirely on Him for our satisfaction. It is only as we know God that our souls can be truly fulfilled. We are no strangers to this truth. We have grown so accustomed to hearing Augustine's classic statement "Because you have made us for Yourself, our hearts are restless till

---

11. For the exegetical and biblical-theological basis for these claims, see G. K. Beale, *The Temple and the Church's Mission: A Biblical Theology of the Dwelling Place of God*, New Studies in Biblical Theology 17, ed. D. A. Carson (Downers Grove, Ill.: InterVarsity, 2004), 29–121.

12. Johannes P. Louw and Eugene A. Nida, *Greek-English Lexicon of the New Testament Based on Semantic Domains* (New York: United Bible Societies, 1998), 13.67.

13. For more on this distinction, see J. I. Packer, *Knowing God* (Downers Grove, Ill.: InterVarsity, 1973), 25–27. Packer writes, "A little knowledge *of* God is worth more than a great deal of knowledge *about* him" (26). Knowing God necessitates that we know about Him. We cannot divorce these two kinds of knowledge, but we must distinguish between them.

they find their rest in Thee" that our eyes glaze over when we encounter it.[14] The Westminster Shorter Catechism's magisterial adage that the chief aim of our existence is "to glorify God, and to enjoy him forever" has become humdrum. But it is here that humility rests its case. The lowly disposition of humility reckons with the reality that only One can truly satisfy the soul. The humble saint pants after the God who is her "exceeding joy" (Ps. 43:4). She declares from the heart, "Whom have I in heaven but You? And there is none upon earth that I desire besides You" (Ps. 73:25). She cries out, "My soul longs, yes, even faints for the courts of the LORD" (Ps. 84:2).

We live in a world desperately pursuing satisfaction in the creature rather than in the Creator. The prideful bent of our hearts makes us averse to depending entirely on God for our joy. We deceive ourselves into believing that if we could merely attain a higher salary, a more impressive position, a prettier girlfriend, a happier marriage, or a healthier body, then we would be truly happy. So we spend our lives pursuing fulfillment where it can never be found.

C. S. Lewis said it well: "Our Lord finds our desires not too strong, but too weak. We are halfhearted creatures, fooling about with drink and sex and ambition when infinite joy is offered us, like an ignorant child who wants to go on making mud pies in a slum because he cannot imagine what is meant by the offer of a holiday at the sea. We are far too easily pleased."[15] And here is the reason you and I spend our days fooling around with mud pies—it is because we are proud. We refuse to accept that, as image of God, we are thoroughly dependent on God for our joy. We refuse the offer of limitless delight in our Creator, preferring the fleeting, futile pleasures of idolatry.

Humility's Realism
As we saw in the last chapter, humility is often defined as Godward dependence. The truths of this chapter serve to explain in part why

14. Augustine, *The Confessions of St. Augustine* (Brewster, Mass.: Paraclete Press, 2006), 1.1.1.
15. C. S. Lewis, *The Weight of Glory and Other Addresses* (Grand Rapids: Eerdmans, 1965), 2.

this is so. The downward disposition of humility is undergirded by a pervasive consciousness of our inescapable creaturely dependence. And that lowly recognition of heart leads to active, willful reliance on God.

The reality is that you are dependent on God for your existence, your identity, and your satisfaction whether you acknowledge it or not. As image, you are and have nothing apart from the Original. There are only two options for you—either happily embrace this reality or live in a self-constructed fairy tale. In our pride, we choose the fairy tale. Just because pride is anti-God, it is anti-reality. It is the outright rejection of our creatureliness. It is the exaltation of the creature over the Creator. Humility, to the contrary, is perfectly realistic. It joyfully upholds the existential gulf between the creature and the Creator. Humility does not have an overly negative view of humankind but simply reckons with what you and I are by nature—creatures entirely dependent on our entirely independent Creator.

CHAPTER 2

Covenantal Creatures

One predominant and often overlooked reason why Christians remain spiritually immature is they fail to consider their creatureliness. The church makes much of sin and Christ, and it ought to. But the fact is, our conception of the fall and the incarnation will never run deeper than our conception of what it is to be a creature. Our creatureliness is foundational to our faith and to our humility. As we saw in the previous chapter, one implication of being a creature is our inescapable dependence on God. Now we turn to a second—our inescapable relation to God.

G. C. Berkouwer perceptively writes, "Scripture is concerned with man in his relation to God, in which he can never be seen as man-in-himself."[1] The Bible never presents humans as humans-in-themselves. It has no category for creatures who are untethered to their Creator. From Genesis to Revelation, humankind is presented as essentially and fundamentally related to God as His image. But it does not stop there, for along with this natural association, God has been pleased to relate to humankind covenantally.

A divine-human covenant is a special relationship sovereignly initiated by God in which He binds His image to Himself. God created man for this very end. No sooner had He formed Adam from

---

1. G. C. Berkouwer, *Man: The Image of God* (Grand Rapids: Eerdmans, 1962), 59–60.

the dust of the ground than He entered into a binding, covenantal relationship with him. Adam was created for covenant.

A Covenant with Adam?

"But wait a minute," you say, "the word *covenant* isn't found in the Bible until Genesis 6:18. Is it not stretching the biblical data to say that God entered into a covenant with Adam when the term is nowhere to be found?"

The point is well taken. The word *covenant* is not present in Genesis 1–2. The absence of the word, however, cannot be equated with the absence of the reality. You will search in vain to find the words *humility* or *humble* in the opening chapters of Genesis, yet we have seen that humility was present and operative from the moment God created man. Similarly, you will not find the words *marriage* or *wedding* in Genesis 2:22–25, but that is precisely what takes place. To argue that a reality cannot be present apart from its corresponding term is a careless form of reasoning.

The word may not be used, but the reality of covenant is most certainly present in the second creation account (Gen. 2:4–17). Here we find God sovereignly entering into a binding relationship with His image-bearing creature. As we will see, this relation placed certain obligations on Adam, holding out blessings to him for fulfilling them and curses for failing to do so. Every element that is indispensable to a biblical covenant is present in the garden.

Furthermore, later Scripture passages affirm that God covenanted with Adam before the fall. Hosea points to Adam's covenant-breaking as paradigmatic for Israel's covenant-breaking: "But like Adam they transgressed the covenant; there they dealt faithlessly with me" (Hos. 6:7 ESV). For Adam to transgress the covenant (a clear reference to the fall into sin), first there had to be a covenant to transgress. The apostle Paul, following Hosea, assumes this to be the case when he draws parallels between Adam and Christ, teaching that Adam did not function as a lone individual in the garden, but as the covenant head of the entire human race (Rom. 5:12–21; 1 Cor. 15:21–22).

God covenanted with Adam at creation. This truth is no mere doctrinal nicety but one of fundamental importance as we seek to understand what it means for us to be creatures. God's covenant has much to teach us about humility. A proper understanding of it, driven home to the heart, will promote within us the downward disposition of a Godward self-perception.

The Creator's Voluntary Condescension

In order for God to relate to creatures by way of covenant, He must first condescend. Westminster Confession 7.1 states that we could know nothing of God apart from "some voluntary condescension on God's part, which he hath been pleased to express by way of covenant." We are all familiar with the word *condescension*, but we typically use it in a negative fashion today.

Down the road from my house is Fairyland Elementary School. When we first moved in, locals kept mentioning "Furlend School." I didn't know what they were talking about.

"Furlend School?" I asked.

"Yes, the elementary school a few miles from your home," was the reply.

"Oh," I said, "you mean, *Fairyland* School?"

"No, *Furlend* School."

Here was my opportunity to teach my Southern neighbor a lesson. Anyone would understand that the school is pronounced *Fair-ee-land*. But giving my newfound acquaintance a lesson in rudimentary English pronunciation was probably not the best way to make a friend. To correct my neighbor by demonstrating my perfect, Northern pronunciation would be to speak condescendingly toward him. It would entail me approaching him with an air of superiority aimed at making him feel dumb. That is typically how we understand condescension. It is standing over people to shame them by drawing attention to their inferiority.[2]

---

2. When I originally used this illustration in preaching, I was informed by one of my listeners that while poking fun at the pronunciation of my Southern

When the Lord condescends, however, He does not stand over us to highlight our inferiority. Instead, He comes down to us to overcome our inferiority. It is God's *descent* that is the essence of His condescending. Notice again how Westminster Confession 7.1 puts it: "The distance between God and the creature is so great, that although reasonable creatures do owe obedience unto him as their Creator, yet they could never have any fruition of him as their blessedness and reward, but by some voluntary condescension on God's part, which he hath been pleased to express by way of covenant."

There is a great distance between us and God. This is not spatial, as if God were billions of miles away. It is not temporal, as if God were living in a different era. The distance is ontological, which is a distance in terms of God's being or essence. God is not like us. He is entirely other than us, so much so that we could know nothing of Him if He did not stoop to our level in order to relate to us in a way accommodated to creatures. John Calvin likens God in His act of revealing Himself to a nurse lisping to a newborn baby.[3] That is precisely what God does in His covenant with us. He lisps. He gets down to our level in order to relate to us.

If I were to address you with the same high-pitched, playful voice with which I speak to my ten-month-old son, you would either be offended or amused. If I were to bury my face behind my jacket, pull it out, and exclaim, "Peek-a-boo!" as we sat over a cup of coffee, you would probably question my mental stability. There is no such distance between you and me, requiring me to condescend in order to relate to you. But the distance between us and God is infinitely great, requiring an infinite descent on His part.

This is a humbling truth. How is it that creatures like us can know God? It is not because we worked our way up to Him. It is only because He has come down to us. We could have no "fruition

---

neighbors, I had mispronounced the word *pronunciation*. After looking into it, I realized I had. My critique of Southern mispronunciation was mispronounced. Sometimes the Lord has humorous ways of humbling us!

3. Calvin, *Institutes*, 1.13.1.

of him as [our] blessedness and reward" apart from His descent. We couldn't know God any more than a toddler could grasp a postdoctoral course on quantum physics. If our Creator didn't get low and lisp to us, we would be in the dark. We are entirely reliant on His voluntary condescension to us. And this is true not because of sin, but because we are creatures. What a lowly spirit this infinite distance and infinite condescension ought to produce in us![4]

The Creator's Absolute Authority

We speak of God's condescension as voluntary because God was not coerced into doing it. No one twisted His arm to relate to us. Remember, God is *a se*. He is the independent Creator who needs nothing and takes orders from no one. So it should not surprise us to find God sovereignly initiating and establishing the terms of His covenant with Adam.

God didn't come down to deliberate with man concerning the covenant. He didn't say, "Adam, I've been thinking about entering into a binding relationship with you as the head of the human race. Do you see that tree? I'm considering making it off-limits in order to test you. What do you think?" A divine-human covenant is not a relationship between two equal parties. God came to Adam as covenant Lord, initiating the relationship with absolute, unqualified authority. No forum was provided for man's input or advice. The creature simply didn't get a say. God spoke, and it was done. And He spoke by way of authoritative command: "Of every tree of the garden you may freely eat; but of the tree of the knowledge of good and evil you shall not eat, for in the day that you eat of it you shall surely die" (Gen. 2:16–17).

Does this not seem like a rather strange arrangement? Why would God forbid His creature to eat of this one tree? We are told later that the tree "was good for food" (Gen. 3:6). God didn't prohibit

---

4. Francis Turretin refers to God's forging of this covenant bond as "his infinite condescension." *Institutes of Elenctic Theology*, trans. George Musgrave Giger, ed. James T. Dennison Jr. (Phillipsburg, N.J.: P&R, 1992), 1:574.

eating from it because its fruit tasted bitter or lacked nutritional value. We are given no indication that there was anything unique about this one tree in itself. Presumably, Adam and Eve found themselves surrounded by hundreds of trees that looked similar.

God's sovereign command by which He initiated covenant with Adam, and us in Adam, appeared arbitrary. That is the precise language of Cornelius Van Til: "God chose one tree from among many and 'arbitrarily' told man not to eat of it."[5] The dictionary defines *arbitrary* as "existing or coming about seemingly at random or by chance."[6] Is it proper to speak of God acting arbitrarily? Surely He does nothing randomly or whimsically. But there are times when God acts in a way that appears arbitrary from the creature's limited perspective.[7]

Think of a father who gives his son a set of wooden blocks for his birthday and then, on dumping them out, says, "My boy, all of these blocks are yours to play with and enjoy, except for this large rectangular one. This block is off-limits." Such a prohibition is bound to elicit the question, "Why, Daddy?" There is nothing special about that block. In fact, there are nineteen others that are identical to it in shape, size, and color. The father's word has every appearance of being random. When God barred Adam from this one tree, it would have appeared the same. Why did God do this?

It is actually the arbitrariness of the command that takes us to the heart of its purpose. The apparent randomness of the prohibition is essential to God's reason for giving it. "In this particular situation," explains O. Palmer Robertson, "man had nothing to indicate the

5. Cornelius Van Til, "Nature and Scripture," in *The Infallible Word: A Symposium by the Members of the Faculty of Westminster Theological Seminary*, ed. N. B. Stonehouse and Paul Woolley, 2nd ed. (Phillipsburg, N.J.: P&R, 1967), 269.

6. *Merriam-Webster's Collegiate Dictionary*, s.v. "arbitrary," accessed September 28, 2021, https://unabridged.merriam-webster.com/collegiate/arbitrary.

7. I believe this is why Van Til puts *arbitrary* in quotation marks. He is not saying God actually acted arbitrarily, but that His command gave every appearance of arbitrariness.

exceptional nature of this one tree other than the word of God."[8] The tree had no intrinsic features distinguishing it from the others. There was nothing peculiar about its appearance or its smell or the taste of its fruit. The only reality setting this tree apart was God's speech. And the question presenting itself to man was, "Will you live in submission to your Creator even when His command appears random? Will you bow in humble obedience simply because that is what creatures do when they encounter the authoritative word of their Creator?"

The arbitrariness of the command served to highlight God's authority as Creator and covenant Lord. Robertson states, "One tree stands in the midst of the garden as symbolic reminder that man is not God."[9] In other words, this tree was a sign and seal of Adam's creatureliness. Every time he would see the tree of the knowledge of good and evil, he would be reminded that he was not free to do as he pleased. As creatures, we are morally bound and accountable to our Creator.[10]

Belief in the existence of absolute moral standards that are universally binding on all people regardless of their subjective opinions and feelings is extremely off-putting in our current cultural moment. The philosopher Charles Taylor puts words to the ethical mantra of our age: "Let each person do their own thing.... One shouldn't criticize the others' values, because they have a right to live their own life as you do."[11] And here is what is so scary: you don't have to bury yourself in some massive philosophical tome to be exposed to these

---

8. O. Palmer Robertson, *The Christ of the Covenants* (Phillipsburg, N.J.: P&R, 1980), 84.

9. Robertson, *Christ of the Covenants*, 83.

10. This truth could have easily been included in the previous chapter. As image-bearing creatures, we were created to reflect God in righteousness and holiness (Eph. 4:24). Adam and Eve had the law written on their hearts and were accountable to live in obedience to God, even apart from this special covenant arrangement. But it was through the initiation of this covenant, with its prohibition, that God more explicitly revealed His authority over the realm of ethics.

11. Charles Taylor, *A Secular Age* (Cambridge, Mass.: Harvard University Press, 2007), 484.

ideas. We find such subjective, relativistic morality everywhere we look. It is even being spoon-fed to our children. Elsa, a character in the popular Disney movie *Frozen*, expresses this postmodern mentality in the song "Let It Go":

> It's time to see what I can do
> To test the limits and break through.
> No right, no wrong, no rules for me.
> I'm free!

In revealing God's unqualified lordship over the ethical realm, the covenant of works clashes with the secular mentality. We are not free to live as we please. At every point we are related to God as both Creator *and* covenant Lord. And His naked word has absolute authority over us. There is right. There is wrong. There are rules. And they are not defined by us. We are creatures! It is the height of creaturely arrogance to declare, "No right, no wrong, no rules for me." But that is precisely what is being celebrated in our culture. Al Mohler notes, "The secular storm we face undercuts all notions of authority, placing on the throne the subjective self—a false notion of liberated humanity freed from the shackles of theism and the biblical worldview."[12] The "subjective self" has been enthroned as ethical lord, and all claims to an outside, transcendent, absolute authority must be silenced. But God's word cannot be muzzled. His covenant speaks loud and clear to the pride paraded about us in this fallen world.

The question is, Will we listen? Will we embrace our creatureliness? Will we submit to God's authoritative word in a spirit of lowliness as Adam and Eve were called to do? The downward disposition of a Godward self-perception enables us to see ourselves as creatures who are at all times and all places under the authority and dominion of our covenant Lord.

---

12. R. Albert Mohler Jr., *The Gathering Storm: Secularism, Culture, and the Church* (Nashville: Nelson Books, 2020), 15.

The Creator's Sober Sanctions

Though the initiation of God's covenant with Adam was one-sided, defined and established by God alone, the maintenance of this relationship was two-sided. Adam now had obligations not to eat of a certain tree. His passivity in the covenant's inauguration led to responsible activity before the Lord. Adam now had a choice. He could either keep covenant by living in creaturely submission to God, or he could break covenant by pridefully eating the forbidden fruit.

As covenant King, God warned Adam of the curse that would come on him if he chose the second route—"in the day that you eat of it you shall surely die" (Gen. 2:17). The language here is emphatic. It literally reads, "Dying you will die."

The curse is not limited to the cessation of bodily life. While it certainly was a warning of the physical mortality that would plague humanity if Adam broke covenant, death is most fundamentally a separation from the source of all life, God Himself.[13] It is a severing of the creature's relation to the Creator. No grimmer prospect is imaginable than this—the image being cut off from the Original, the creature coming under the wrath of the Creator. The emphatic sanction of death was nothing short of eternal death, the loss of loving communion with God.

Does this all seem a bit over the top? What father strikes his daughter dead for catching her with her hand in the cookie jar? Eternal death merely for eating a piece of fruit?

We need to recognize that this was no mere eating fruit. If Adam took from this tree, he would be despising the word of his sovereign. Before he could eat it, he first had to rise up in autonomous revolt against his Lord. As we will explore in greater detail in the pages

---

13. John Murray writes that the death threatened here "has a threefold aspect, spiritual (moral and religious, judicial, and psycho-physical)." He goes on to explain, "Spiritual death describes man's moral and religious condition; judicial death describes his status with reference to God; psycho-physical death describes the disruption of his very being." "The Adamic Administration," in *Collected Writings of John Murray* (Edinburgh: Banner of Truth, 1977), 2:56–57.

ahead, to eat from the tree would actually be a rejection of his creatureliness. Pride is the illusion that we are sovereign.

The fruit was not the issue. The issue was whether the image
would live in humble submission to the Original. And it was an issue
of life and death. God warned Adam of what would happen if he
began to perceive himself as "man-in-himself." To deny the Creator
and deify the creature would result in death. To exclaim, "No right,
no wrong, no rules for me. I'm free!" was the road to hell. Pride is
such an abomination to God that it warrants the sword of His eternal judgment.

What we often fail to see, however, is that God not only set forth
curses for covenant-breaking, but He also assured of blessings for
covenant-keeping. Westminster Confession 7.2 asserts that "life was
promised to Adam; and in him to his posterity" through this binding
arrangement. Implicit in God's warning of death was the promise of
life. If Adam walked humbly with his covenant Lord, then he would
be confirmed in a state of sinless life in God's presence.

This extension of life to Adam on the condition of humble obedience was represented in the tree of life (Gen. 2:9). The tree had
no magical power to confer life. The everlasting life promised in
the covenant was found in God alone. But similar to the way that
partaking of the Lord's Supper signifies and seals to Christians the
life they have only in Christ, the tree of life signified and confirmed
eternal life to its partakers. It functioned sacramentally, being a God-
ordained, visible sign of an invisible, spiritual reality. And that is why
God was so quick to bar Adam from it after he broke covenant (3:22).
If Adam would only walk in humility before his fatherly Creator,
then life—everlasting life—was his for the taking.

The more we understand what it is to be a creature, the more
this promise of life will amaze us. The Creator-creature distinction
makes clear that this blessedness being held out to us in Adam is
entirely a gift. The creature is required to render perfect obedience
to his Creator, but God as covenant Lord is not required to lavish
the creature with blessing. For "who has first given to Him and it
shall be repaid to him?" (Rom. 11:35). The obvious answer is *no one.*

A servant does not deserve to be showered with his master's riches simply for doing his duty. God doesn't owe His creature anything. He is no debtor. What grounds for humility this is! After having done our duty, we are still "unworthy servants" (Luke 17:10 ESV). But in His large-hearted goodness, the Creator Lord holds out unspeakable blessing to us.

Covenantal Humility

No matter who you are, you are in covenant with your Creator. When God condescended to covenant with Adam, He covenanted with all humankind in him. All of us are born in a binding relationship with God as our sovereign Lord.

Sit on a park bench and watch the multitudes pass by. The sophisticated businesswoman on her cell phone, the frazzled mother attempting to calm her screaming toddler, the homeless beggar asking for your change, the young couple delightedly holding hands— all of them are covenanted to their Creator. No man is a man-in-himself. No woman is a woman-in-herself. We are at all times and in all places inescapably related to God.

Understanding and embracing our identity as covenantal creatures is essential to growing downward in humility. We simply cannot have a Godward self-perception without knowledge of the covenant. We don't work our way to God; He comes down to us. We don't set the terms of our relationship with God; He sovereignly establishes His relation with us. We aren't the definers of the moral order; God is. We owe everything to our Creator; He owes nothing to us. Could there be greater warrant for a lowly spirit than these truths?

The creature's inescapable covenant bond to the Creator teaches us that true freedom is found only as we bow under God's absolute authority over our every act, word, thought, and desire. Autonomy leads to death.[14] Humility leads to life. Which path will you choose?

---

14. *Autonomy* is creatures' groundless assumption that they are not accountable to their Creator but are a law unto themselves (i.e., self-rule). To sing, "No rules for me, I'm free" really means, "I'm in charge. I call the shots. I'm king."

CHAPTER 3

Temporal Creatures

I am thirty years old. Three decades have come and gone in the blink of an eye, leaving a series of ever-fading memories in their wake. And the clock is not slowing down. As the old hymn puts it:

> Time, like an ever-rolling stream,
> Bears all its sons away;
> They fly forgotten, as a dream
> Dies at the op'ning day.[1]

Though we often don't like to admit it, we are sons and daughters of this "ever-rolling stream" called *time*. You and I are time bound. We exist within a never-resting temporal sequence that is swiftly moving toward the grave. In a later chapter we will explore the theme of death, but first we must grapple with our temporality. Few realities serve to give us a controlling sense of our creatureliness like our inescapable relation to time.

Eternal Creator, Temporal Creatures

The Bible begins at the beginning. In fact, those are its first three words—"In the beginning" (Gen. 1:1). What does a beginning require in order to begin? Most fundamentally, it requires time. A beginning cannot happen apart from some kind of temporal sequence. To put

---

1. Isaac Watts, "Our God, Our Help in Ages Past," in the public domain.

it another way, without a succession of moments, you cannot have a first moment. Genesis records for us the very first moment of history. And notice, God was already there. "In the beginning God…" (v. 1). God never began to be. He is "the everlasting God" (Isa. 40:28). Getting your mind around God's eternality is like trying to wrap your arms around Mount Everest. It is simply impossible. "Behold, God is great, and we do not know Him; nor can the number of His years be discovered" (Job 36:26). When the Bible attributes years to God (cf. Ps. 102:27), it is not speaking literally. In revealing Himself, God lisps. He gets down on our creaturely level, speaking of His timelessness in the categories of time. Time-bound creatures have no ability to think of existence apart from a temporal sequence of some kind. But God's eternality means that He exists outside of and above time. When the psalmist says He is "from everlasting to everlasting" (Ps. 90:2), he does not mean that there is an infinite succession of moments in God. He is worshiping the God whose supreme existence is independent of time altogether. As Anselm states, "Now, although without you nothing can exist, you are not in space or time but all things are in you. For you are not contained by anything but rather you contain all things."[2] Nothing contains God—not time, not space. He is "I Am" (Ex. 3:14).

The opening words of the Bible confront us with a profound mystery, however. While God is boundless, subsisting apart from the limitations of spatial and temporal existence, He yet possesses the ability to create the space-time universe and relate to it.[3] The eternal God creates. He causes the beginning to be, and then He fashions a world full of creatures within this temporal sequence.

While the Creator is necessarily eternal, creatures are necessarily temporal. To be a creature is to have a beginning and to exist in a series of temporal moments. It is simply impossible for a creature to

---

2. Anselm, *Monologion and Proslogion, with the Replies of Gaunilo and Anselm*, trans. Thomas Williams (Indianapolis: Hackett, 1996), 106.
3. For more on this, see James E. Dolezal, *All That Is in God: Evangelical Theology and the Challenge of Classical Christian Theism* (Grand Rapids: Reformation Heritage Books, 2017), 79–104.

exist outside the confines of time. Our temporality is an exclamation point on our creatureliness. Herman Bavinck writes, "One who says 'time' says motion, change, measurability, computability, limitation, finiteness, creature."[4] To exist in time is to be finite, limited, and ever changing. Our seconds, minutes, hours, days, and years serve as a continual reminder that we are not God. We are not limitless creators; we are limited creatures.

Creaturely Limitations Day by Day

I found him on a concrete slab outside of the dorm at 2:30 a.m., lying facedown in a puddle of drool. "Come on, you sluggard! This is no time to be sleeping!" I thought to myself as I shook him awake. Why was I irritated with my friend? He was supposed to be praying! We had been zealously seeking the Lord together, rising in the middle of the night to pray for revival. This was doable for one night, but as the weeks stretched on, it became unsustainable. We pushed and pushed, but eventually our bodies collapsed. Our zeal for the Lord was undergirded by the false notion that sleep was unspiritual and a waste of time. Our unspoken motto was, "While mediocre Christians sleep, mighty Christians weep. While mediocre Christians snore, mighty Christians implore." We had forgotten we were creatures.

Limited by Twenty-Four Hours

One of the first truths the Bible confronts us with is that God not only created time but also structured it. Having spoken light into the darkness, God separated a period of light from a period of darkness, designating these periods *day* and *night* (Gen. 1:3–5). Later, God created the sun and moon to govern this twenty-four-hour sequence of light and darkness (vv. 14–19). Contrary to evolutionary theory, it is no random accident that the earth revolves around the sun with such perfect precision so as to bring about this temporal cycle. The

---

4. Herman Bavinck, *Reformed Dogmatics*, ed. John Bolt, trans. John Vriend (Grand Rapids: Baker Academic, 2004), 2:163.

fact that our days consist of exactly twenty-four hours of light and darkness is by divine design.

If I may be frank with you, sometimes I don't like the temporal structure God has designed. I long for a world in which days are forty-eight hours long. I dream of sci-fi planets furnished with time-stopping devices. Wouldn't it be something to be able to halt the clock, make the sun stand still, and extend a day as long as you wish—all at the click of a button? Imagine what you could accomplish. Imagine how successful and productive you could be. You would be limitless.

Ah, there it is. Limitless.

Why do I dislike the temporal structure God has designed? Because it is constantly confronting me with my limitations.[5] I don't like to be ruled by day and night. I want to be in charge. I don't like being confined to twenty-four-hour days. I want to be free from any kind of temporal constraints. To put the matter simply, I want to be God.

When the pressures of life or the aspirations of the heart lead us to exclaim in frustration, "I don't have enough time!" we are despising our creatureliness. We are saying, "I want to be the eternal Creator, not a time-bound creature." But that is precisely the opposite of what God intended when He structured our days. God's gracious intention was that, instead of hardening us in pride, our temporal limitations would foster the downward disposition of a Godward self-perception. Far from hating limitations, humility joyfully embraces them. It recognizes that temporal boundaries come with the territory of creaturehood.[6]

---

5. I am indebted to Paul David Tripp for his comments on the limitations of time in *Lead: 12 Gospel Principles for Leadership in the Church* (Wheaton, Ill.: Crossway, 2020), 77–80.

6. God is not only limitless temporally but also spatially. This week, I drove five hours to a presbytery meeting in North Carolina. God was present at the meeting, but unlike me, He didn't have to travel to get there. God never has to travel to get anywhere. The Creator is not bound by the spatial limitations of the creature. Have you ever considered that seemingly pointless activities like

Limited by Sleep

The boundaries we face are actually much narrower than first meets the eye. Yes, you exist within a twenty-four-hour, temporal framework of day and night. But the reality is that as a creature, you will occupy roughly a third of that time lying on a mattress in the dark. Consider for a moment that if you get the medically recommended eight hours of sleep per night, you will spend approximately three thousand hours a year in bed. That is 180,000 minutes!

Like many in our fast-paced, caffeinated age, you might think, "Eight hours a night? Who has time for that? You clearly don't understand how busy my life is." To which I respond, "No, you clearly don't understand your limitations."

You actually need seven to eight hours of quality sleep every night to thrive as a human being. To neglect this creaturely necessity brings devastating consequences. Matthew Walker, the director of the Center for Human Sleep Science, writes, "No facet of the human body is spared the crippling, noxious harm of sleep loss. We are… socially, organizationally, economically, physically, behaviorally, nutritionally, linguistically, cognitively, and emotionally dependent upon sleep."[7]

We could add *spiritually* to this list. Have you ever tried listening to biblical preaching or praying or loving your children or serving your spouse after getting only four hours of sleep the night before? It is extremely difficult to love God and other people when we are sleep deprived. As creatures, our spiritual life is tethered to our physical life. That is why when my friend and I consistently sought to deprive ourselves of sleep in order to pray, very little praying actually occurred. God isn't pleased when our approach to His throne of grace ends in a subconscious pool of drool.

---

your morning commute to work or school are actually God-ordained reminders of your creatureliness? We ought to seize on these spatial limitations to cultivate humility.

7. Matthew Walker, *Why We Sleep: Unlocking the Power of Sleep and Dreams* (New York: Scribner, 2017), 133.

When I neglect sleep, I am far more prone to worry, depression, overeating, irritability, rash decision-making, and a long list of other traits unbefitting of a Christian. For years I struggled with significant social anxiety. Sometimes I would be so gripped by nervousness that I could hardly breathe, let alone get words out of my mouth. At the same time, I was purposefully neglecting sleep, getting an average of four to six hours per night. It never crossed my mind that there might be a connection between my social anxiety and my sleep deficiency. After all, I thought, who needs eight hours of sleep when you have the Holy Spirit? But when I finally came to see the premium the Scriptures place on the bodily dimension of our creaturely existence, I began to prioritize sleep (along with diet and exercise). And do you know what happened to my anxiety? It largely disappeared.[8]

There is no facet of your creaturely existence that is not dependent on sleep. If you attempt to run unremittingly, it will result in significant—even potentially irreparable—breakdown. But that is how many of us live our lives. We often practically deny our temporal finitude. And it is pride.

John Piper likens sleep to "a broken record" playing the same old message night after night. What is that message? "Man is not sovereign. Man is not sovereign. Man is not sovereign."[9] Consider the most powerful people on the planet—the president of the United States, the CEO of Amazon, the dictator of China. Even they must come to the end of the day, put on their pajamas, crawl into bed, and drift off into dreamland. Even they, with all their splendor, must daily subject themselves to a most helpless condition wherein their exercise of oversight, power, protection, and production comes to a

---

8. Anxiety is a complex problem and each case needs to be treated with special care. I'm in no way asserting here that all anxiety is the result of insufficient sleep. That is definitely not the case. I'm merely pointing to my personal experience to show that when we fail to reckon with our temporal limitations, it can lead to any number of crippling physical, psychological, and spiritual conditions, including anxiety.

9. John Piper, "A Brief Theology of Sleep," Articles, Desiring God, August 3, 1982, http://www.desiringgod.org/articles/a-brief-theology-of-sleep/.

screeching halt. For all their impressive strength, they cannot escape their creatureliness.

There is only One who grows neither weary nor weak (Isa. 40:28). There is only One who neither slumbers nor sleeps (Ps. 121:4). He is God, and He lulls us to sleep each night in order to deliver us from our self-deifying propensities. Every evening as we lay our heads to rest, He graciously confronts us with our creaturely finitude.[10]

Are you seizing your sleep to cultivate humility? Are you using your mattress to grow in the downward disposition of a Godward self-perception? As you close your eyes each night, pray, "Lord, what limitations I have! How quickly a day's work wears me out. By embracing Your gift of sleep, I relinquish my illusion of control. I look to You as the keeper of my soul, my family, my church, my all. You who neither slumber nor sleep, be my keeper this night." When your alarm clock goes off in the morning, give thanks to the God who "gives His beloved sleep" (Ps. 127:2). Thank Him for refreshing you in your creaturely weakness. Praise Him as the One who has kept you through

---

10. Recently, I have been struggling with bouts of mild insomnia. I'm not purposefully neglecting sleep. I want to sleep. I recognize my creaturely need of sleep. But I find myself waking up at 1:00 a.m., feeling like I drank five cups of coffee! Then the sermon I need to prepare or the difficult counseling session scheduled for the next day comes to mind, and I think, "How am I ever going to do this without a good night of rest?" My thoughts produce anxiety, and my restless heart further inhibits me from falling back to sleep. It is pride and a lack of a Godward self-perception. It is an attempt to control what is outside of my control. God is the one who gives sleep, so why not ask Him for it? God is the one who gives sleep, so why not rest in the truth that He knows precisely how much I need to do the work He has called me to tomorrow? God knows my creaturely limitations far better than I do, and sometimes He takes sleep away in order to teach me to surrender to and depend on Him. I have found particular comfort in memorizing Psalm 131 and reciting it in the watches of the night. This psalm has served to put my heart to rest, thereby lulling me to sleep. If you struggle with insomnia (and even if you don't), I highly recommend memorizing this short psalm along with reading David Powlison's article "'Peace, be still': Learning Psalm 131 by Heart," *The Journal of Biblical Counseling* 18, no. 3 (Spring 2000): 2–9. It can be found online at https://www.ccef.org/wp-content/uploads/2016/09/Peace-be-still-Learning-Psalm-131-by-Heart.pdf.

another night. God has ordained sleep so that you might begin and end every day with a controlling sense of your creatureliness.

Creaturely Limitations Week by Week

Our days are structured to serve as a continual reminder that we are not the Creator, and so too are our weeks. God could have instantaneously created everything. But He didn't choose to do that. Instead, He created over a period of six days (Gen. 1:3–2:1). Having spoken the entirety of created existence into being, God then ceased His creational labors on day 7: "And on the seventh day God ended His work which He had done, and He rested on the seventh day from all His work which He had done" (2:2).

Why did God rest? Was He worn out from the difficult work of speaking galaxies into existence? Did the formation of billions of stars and innumerable grains of sand tax His strength? Certainly not.

The everlasting God, the LORD,
The Creator of the ends of the earth,
Neither faints nor is weary. (Isa. 40:28)

So why would God choose to work six days and rest one? He was providing a temporal pattern for His image to reflect. This is made clear in Genesis 2:3: "Then God blessed the seventh day and sanctified it, because in it He rested from all His work which God had created and made." The first created thing ever to be declared holy was a day. By resting on, blessing, and sanctifying the seventh day, God was instituting the Sabbath. This sacred day of rest did not commence with Moses on Mount Sinai; it had its beginnings with God at the inception of space and time. That is why when God gives the fourth commandment to Israel hundreds of years later, He roots the Sabbath command in creation: "For in six days the LORD made the heavens and the earth, the sea, and all that is in them, and rested the seventh day. Therefore the LORD blessed the Sabbath day and hallowed it" (Ex. 20:11). God structured the creational week as a pattern for His image-bearing creatures to follow, working six days and resting one.

As we saw in chapter 1, images are always defined by the original. If I hold up a portrait of George Washington and matter-of-factly assert, "This is Leonardo da Vinci's *Mona Lisa*," you would probably encourage me to go to the eye doctor. A picture that looks nothing like da Vinci's famous painting cannot claim to be its image. For an image to be legitimate, it must reflect the original. It is the same with us. God created us to be a creaturely copy, or reflection, of Him. By working six days and resting one, the Original was giving a temporal structure for His image to mimic. The Sabbath, writes John Murray, "would advise [man] that his life in this world was patterned after the divine example."[11] The weekly structure of our temporal existence is a constant reminder that we are image-bearing creatures, defined by and dependent on the Original at every point. And this, of course, is intended to produce within us the downward disposition of a Godward self-perception.

The Lord Is My Sovereign

By resting God was taking His seat on the throne of creation. His rest is a revelation of His sovereignty. Throughout the Old Testament, the temple is called the place of God's rest. David refers to it as "a house of rest for the ark of the covenant of the LORD, and for the footstool of our God" (1 Chron. 28:2). The psalmist declares,

Let us go into His tabernacle;
Let us worship at His footstool.
Arise, O LORD, to Your resting place. (Ps. 132:7–8)

The temple was not a celestial bedroom furnished with a plush mattress, Egyptian cotton sheets, and blackout curtains. As the place of God's rest, the temple was where He was enthroned between the cherubim as the King of His people.

When God rested on the seventh day of the creation week, He sat down on the throne of His cosmic temple.

11. John Murray, *Principles of Conduct*, 33.

Thus says the LORD:
"Heaven is My throne,
And earth is My footstool.
Where is the house that you will build Me?
And where is the place of My rest?" (Isa. 66:1)

As King of creation, God entered into "a royal resting in king-dom sovereignty."[12] His rest was not a sign of His weariness, but of His reign.

This reality is made even clearer when we behold the eter-nal Sabbath rest obtained by Jesus Christ. From the apostolic era onward, the church has celebrated the Sabbath on the first day of the week (Sunday) instead of the last (Saturday). Why? Because of the monumental significance of Christ's resurrection on the first day of the week. Just as God entered into kingly rest after completing His work of creation, so too Jesus entered into kingly rest after complet-ing His work of redemption. Having accomplished our salvation, He now sits enthroned over the new creation at His Father's right hand. His is "a royal resting in kingdom sovereignty." Every Sunday (what the New Testament calls the Lord's Day) we are reminded of who truly reigns.

When we keep the Sabbath, we are submitting to the unquali-fied lordship of the triune God over both the original creation and the new creation. God is the Lord of our schedules, the definer of our work and rest, and the determiner of how we spend our days. He is reigning over our temporal existence. He is the sovereign, not us. Every time we look at our calendar with its inevitable seven-day-a-week structure, we ought to remember that we are subjects of the One who alone is free from the strictures of time.

The Lord Is My Sustainer

You and I live in a hyperproductive age that promotes seven-day workweeks that serve the idol of success. A number of years ago, the

---

12. Meredith G. Kline, *Kingdom Prologue: Genesis Foundations for a Cove-nantal Worldview* (Eugene, Ore.: Wipf & Stock, 2006), 35.

billionaire Bill Gates was asked the reason for his rejection of God. His response? "Just in terms of allocation of time resources, religion is not very efficient," he said. "There's a lot more I could be doing on a Sunday morning."[13] We might blush at such candid arrogance, but if we are honest, we sometimes agree that in terms of "time resources," the Sabbath is not very efficient. Imagine how much more work you could accomplish and how much more money you could obtain if only you could work on Sunday.

The apparent inefficiency of the Sabbath is designed to turn our eyes to our all-sufficient God. When deadlines are approaching, when bills are piling up, when projects are unfinished, and when expectations of superiors are mounting, we have the opportunity to declare on the Lord's Day that our trust is not in our creaturely labor. Christian counselor Robert Shaw explains, "When we cease from pursuing our material goals for one day each week, we're saying, 'God, I trust You to maintain control while I spend this day focusing on You. I trust You to provide for my needs seven days a week even if I only work for six of them. Regardless of how much money I could earn today, or how much remains on my to-do list from last week, today I'm going to rest my mind and body and bask in Your presence.'"[14]

God expected Israel to keep the Sabbath even before He gave the law at Sinai. When He rained down bread from heaven each morning, He commanded the people to gather only enough for that day (Ex. 16:16). That changed on the sixth day, however. On Friday they were to gather twice as much so that they could cease from gathering on the Sabbath (vv. 22–26). When the seventh day rolled around, however, some of the Israelites went out to gather, thinking they could store up some extra food (v. 27). And this resulted in the rebuke of the Lord: "See! For the LORD has given you the Sabbath; therefore He gives you on the sixth day bread for two days. Let every

---

13. See Walter Isaacson, "In Search of the Real Bill Gates," *Time* (January 13, 1997): 7.

14. Robert B. Shaw Jr., "Purpose of Sabbath Rest," American Association of Christian Counselors, http://www.aacc.net/2016/07/22/purpose-of-sabbath-rest/.

man remain in his place; let no man go out of his place on the seventh day" (v. 29).

What exactly was happening here? God had given them all that they needed in the space of six workdays. They didn't go out to gather on the seventh because they were famished; they went out because they wanted the comfort of knowing there was a little extra food in the pantry. Then they wouldn't have to live in absolute dependence on God the following day. But God says, "No! No! No! Don't you get it? You are a dependent creature. I will take care of you. Trust Me and rest."

The humble trust God with their financial needs. They trust God to put food on the table seven days a week, even though they work for only six. They trust God with the deadlines and unhealthy expectations of their employers. Humility rests on the Sabbath, looking to God as sustainer.

The Lord Is My Satisfaction
What does it mean for God to bless and sanctify the seventh day (Gen. 2:3)? When God blesses something, He showers it with blessing. When God sanctifies something, He sets it apart as devoted to His service. The reason the Lord's Day is blessed is because it is sanctified for God's worship. It is God's day, devoted to His praise.

Have you ever thought about the fact that Adam and Eve's first full day on this earth was the Sabbath? According to Thomas Boston, the reason for this was "that [Adam] might know the great end of his creation was to serve the Lord."[15] God desired our first parents to know that their ultimate joy and satisfaction were to be found in Him and His worship. And this was before sin. If prefall man needed a day to rest from his earthly vocation in order to be absorbed in the worship of God, how much more so do corrupt creatures like us?

---

15. Thomas Boston, *An Illustration of the Doctrines of the Christian Religion*, in *The Complete Works of Thomas Boston* (Stoke-on-Trent, UK: Tentmaker, 2002), 2:190.

Our prideful hearts are always seeking satisfaction in created things rather than in the Creator. But on the Sabbath, we declare that God is our chief treasure and joy. This is the essence of humility. The downward disposition of a Godward self-perception delights in the beauty of God and desires nothing above Him. It exclaims, "My soul will not be satisfied with earthly riches and human accolades. There is only One who can fill my hungry soul—God!" When we keep the Sabbath holy, we are depending on God to delight our souls in a way nothing else can.

Humbled by Time

Humility pervades our days and weeks. In His perfect wisdom, God not only designed our persons as image bearers and our covenantal relation with Him to promote humility, but He also fashioned the temporal structure of our existence to promote humility. Every day we are confronted with our creaturely limitation and finitude. Every night we are confronted with our creaturely weakness and insufficiency. Every week we are confronted with our creaturely call to image our Creator. Every Sabbath we are confronted with our creaturely dependence on God as our sovereign, sustainer, and satisfaction.

What a mercy this is for our natively haughty hearts! What profound lessons there are to learn about our creatureliness from our clocks and calendars. Time-bound creatures before an eternal Creator—that is what we are. Let us never despise it. Let us embrace our temporality in the pursuit of humility.

PART 2

Ethical Humility

ethical: pertaining to morality or right and wrong
We are fallen, delusional, and helpless sinners.

CHAPTER 4

Fallen Sinners

In his classic work *Christianity and Liberalism*, J. Gresham Machen writes, "At the very root of the modern liberal movement is the loss of the consciousness of sin.... The fundamental fault of the modern Church is that she is busily engaged in an absolutely impossible task—she is busily engaged in calling the righteous to repentance. Modern preachers are trying to bring men into the Church without requiring them to relinquish their pride; they are trying to help men avoid the conviction of sin."[1] That was true in the 1920s, and it continues to be true. Many people in the church desire a religion that brings comfort apart from conviction. They want a religion that builds up apart from tearing down. But Christianity cannot live where there is the denial of humankind's universal depravity. That is why Machen argued that liberalism, with its proclamation of humankind's inherent goodness, is not a malformed Christianity but an entirely different religion altogether.

People who have a Godward self-perception perceive themselves as radically corrupt. While our creatureliness is the ultimate reality impelling us to lowliness (existential humility), our corruption beckons us lower still (ethical humility). If we would possess the downward disposition of humility, we need a pervasive consciousness of our sin.

---

1. J. Gresham Machen, *Christianity and Liberalism*, 2nd ed. (Grand Rapids: Eerdmans, 2009), 55, 58.

Holy Creator, Unholy Creatures

It is not difficult to call to mind examples from redemptive history of God's holy presence invoking such a controlling sense of corruption. Before the smoke-filled, thunder-provoking glory of God at Sinai, the Israelites quaked in fear, entreating their mediator, "You speak with us, and we will hear; but let not God speak with us, lest we die" (Ex. 20:19). With his boat sinking from a miraculous catch of fish, Peter fell before the majestic Christ, crying out, "Depart from me, for I am a sinful man, O Lord!" (Luke 5:8). For postfall creatures, beholding God in His holiness always entails being exposed in our filth. Of all the people we could consider in the Scriptures to see this, however, the prophet Isaiah serves as the example par excellence.

A Controlling Sense of God's Holiness

In the midst of a royal funeral, Isaiah was given a vision of the supreme King. Don't skim over these words because you are familiar with them. Notice what the prophet saw: "In the year that King Uzziah died, I saw the Lord sitting on a throne, high and lifted up, and the train of His robe filled the temple" (Isa. 6:1). Isaiah beheld majesty of the highest sort—an exalted King in regal robes on a royal throne.

The God in Isaiah's vision is breathtakingly high, and Isaiah cannot behold Him without being overtaken by a controlling sense of His majesty. In fact, Isaiah was so overtaken by the divine majesty that he later wrote, "All nations before Him are as nothing, and they are counted by Him less than nothing and worthless" (Isa. 40:17). Take *Time* magazine's "100 Most Influential People," combining all of their talent, intelligence, wealth, and power, and Isaiah says that they are "less than nothing and worthless" before the King of heaven. Talk about a controlling sense of God's majesty!

And that is only the beginning of the vision, for the transcendent Lord was surrounded by an angelic host ceaselessly crying out in adoring worship: "Holy, holy, holy is the LORD of hosts; the whole earth is full of His glory!" (Isa. 6:2–3). Similar to how we use exclamation points in English, Hebrew employs repetition to raise something to the level of a superlative. This threefold repetition indicates that God is holy to the highest degree possible. The question is, What does *holy* mean, especially when it is attributed to God? It is quite common to define God's holiness as His separateness. As the uncreated One, God is separate from everything in creation. As the perfectly pure One, He is separate from everything sinful. These statements are certainly true, but they fall short of getting at the precise nature of God's holiness. Why? Just ask yourself, was God holy before He created the world? Was He holy before the fall into sin? The obvious answer is yes. Herein lies the problem with defining God's holiness as separateness. Separation requires something to be separate from. But before creation, there was nothing created for Him to be separate from. And before the fall, there was nothing sinful for Him to be separate from. Before the beginning of the time-space universe, there was nothing except God. So if God's holiness preceded the creation and fall, then holiness cannot be conceived as separateness. There is no separation in God Himself. The three persons of the Godhead have eternally existed in perfectly interpenetrating communion. And actually, that interpenetration, rather than separation, is the key to understanding the divine holiness.

When a person or object was made holy in the Old Testament, it was set apart. But this was no general or undefined consecration. To be holy was to be set apart *to God.* When Israel was made a holy nation or the tabernacle was consecrated as the holy place, these objects became devoted to God. This leads Sinclair Ferguson rightly to describe God's holiness as "the perfectly pure devotion of each of these three persons to the other two...absolute, permanent, exclusive, pure, irreversible, and fully expressed devotion."[2] God's holiness is essentially His devotion to Himself. While affirming the traditional definition of holiness, Geerhardus Vos agrees by calling it "that attribute of God by which He seeks and loves Himself as the highest good."[3] As the only uncreated One, God loves Himself supremely.

---

2. Sinclair B. Ferguson, *Devoted to God: Blueprints for Sanctification* (Edinburgh: Banner of Truth, 2016), 2. I am indebted to Ferguson for much of what is said here regarding the holiness of God.

3. Vos, *Reformed Dogmatics*, 1:27. Jonathan Edwards argues similarly that

As the perfectly sinless One, God loves Himself supremely. Separation is not essential to God's holiness, for such would make Him dependent on that from which He is separate. Separation is simply the necessary outworking of the incomprehensible and unparalleled love within the triune God as He relates to creation and corruption.

Before marriage Tessa and I never kissed each other. In our culture it is tradition for the wedding ceremony to conclude with the minister joyously declaring, "You may now kiss your bride." But Tessa and I decided not to kiss during the ceremony. Why not? It was not because we believed it would be immoral to publicly express our love in this way. But for us, the first time our lips locked was simply too sacred for the eyes of others to behold.[4]

That is why the seraphim were shielding their faces (Isa. 6:2). There was such sacred energy and bright intensity to this holy love of God that creaturely eyes could not gaze on it. Before the holy One, creatures must erect a barrier, separating themselves lest they be consumed.

Isaiah could not behold this vision without being overcome by "the controlling sense of the majesty and holiness of God and the profound reverence which this apprehension elicits." That, as you may recall, is John Murray's definition of the fear of God.[5] And as Isaiah grew upward in fear, he grew downward in humility. He could not see God in His majesty and holiness without seeing his own creatureliness and corruption, especially his corruption.

A Controlling Sense of Personal Corruption
With God's thrice-holy brilliance beaming on his soul, Isaiah cried out in horror,

---

divine holiness "consist[s] in his love." "Treatise on Grace," in *The Works of Jonathan Edwards*, vol. 21, *Writings on the Trinity, Grace, and Faith*, ed. Sang Hyun Lee (New Haven, Conn.: Yale University Press, 2003), 186.

4. I am adapting an illustration given by Ferguson. *Devoted to God*, 3.

5. John Murray, *Principles of Conduct*, 236. See the introduction for a further discussion of the fear of God in its relation to humility.

Woe is me, for I am undone!
Because I am a man of unclean lips,
And I dwell in the midst of a people of unclean lips;
For my eyes have seen the King,
The LORD of hosts. (Isa. 6:5)

Isaiah had declared woes on God's sinful people (e.g., 5:8, 11, 18, 20), but now he pronounces doom on himself. "In this one piercing utterance," writes E. J. Young, "lies [Isaiah's] whole self-condemnation."[6] What was the reason for his self-denunciation? We aren't left to wonder. "For I am undone! Because I am a man of unclean lips." Isaiah was seeing his sin. His collision with the God of glory resulted in him being decimated by the controlling apprehension of his own depravity. R. C. Sproul explains, "As long as Isaiah could compare himself to other mortals, he was able to sustain a lofty opinion of his own character. The instant he measured himself by the ultimate standard, he was destroyed—morally and spiritually annihilated."[7]

In this traumatic moment, Isaiah's attention was drawn specifically to the corruption of his lips. As he heard the angelic host declaring the praises of God with holy lips, he recognized that such adoring worship was the only rightful response in the King's presence. But unlike the lips of these angelic beings, Isaiah's lips were corrupt. They were not fit for worship or for loving communication with God. And such was true not only of Isaiah but of the entire nation that God had called to declare His praise.[8] This absolutely shattered Isaiah.

The prophet came to recognize that his sin was an infinite affront against an infinitely holy God, warranting infinite wrath and woe. In other words, Isaiah was humbled. Seeing his sinful self before a holy God produced within him a lowly spirit. Here we are given a window into the downward disposition of a Godward self-perception.

---

6. Edward J. Young, *The Book of Isaiah* (Grand Rapids: Eerdmans, 1965), 1:247.

7. R. C. Sproul, *The Holiness of God*, 2nd ed. (Carol Stream, Ill.: Tyndale, 1998), 28.

8. Young, *Book of Isaiah*, 1:248.

For image-bearing creatures living after the fall, the profound lowliness of humility is produced in part by a controlling sense of our own corruption.

Adam's Fall and Our Own

In order to understand that corruption, we need to rewind a few millennia and return to the garden of Eden. The garden has taught us a lot about our creatureliness. Sadly, there are also foundational lessons to be learned there about our corruption.

As we have seen, our first parents were created in humility. They were perfectly depending on, submitting to, and delighting in God. They were humble creatures living in reverential love toward their Father, and they were related to God covenantally. The Lord had condescended to enter into a special relationship with Adam as the head of the human race by way of a prohibition: "Of every tree of the garden you may freely eat; but of the tree of the knowledge of good and evil you shall not eat, for in the day that you eat of it you shall surely die" (Gen. 2:16–17). Were Adam to obey, he would have obtained for himself and all his children everlasting life, but disobedience would result in death—physically, spiritually, and eternally.

It was on what was most likely the first Sabbath day that a dagger was plunged into the downward disposition of man's soul. Humility died—and it died because Adam and Eve cast off their controlling sense of creatureliness. That is essentially what the fall into sin was all about: man seeking to live as though he were the Creator, not the creature.

The Anatomy of the First Temptation

On that fateful day, a serpent lurked in the garden (Gen. 3:1). This was no ordinary snake, but Satan, a guardian angel who had fallen from his high estate. What was the cause of his fall? Pride. Here was God's verdict on Satan: "Your heart was lifted up because of your beauty; you corrupted your wisdom for the sake of your splendor" (Ezek. 28:17). Rather than delighting in God, Satan exulted in his own beauty. Rather than embracing God's wisdom, Satan became wise in his own eyes. Rather than submitting to God's authority, Satan rebelled. Now this fallen angel drew near to our first parents in the form of a serpent, and he drew near with a question.

Satan asked Eve, "Has God indeed said, 'You shall not eat of every tree of the garden'?" (Gen. 3:1). Here is the first recorded question in the history of the world, and it was aimed at God's speech. In his pride, the serpent was attempting to plant seeds of doubt in Eve's mind concerning her Creator. The words may appear to be that of honest inquiry, but that is just what gives them their force, for they are fit to deceive.

The crucial word in Satan's supposed quotation of God is *every*. According to the serpent, God's prohibition was all-encompassing—any and all trees were off-limits. By his question, he sought to make God appear overly restrictive. God had created a vast garden with many trees for Adam and Eve to enjoy, but Satan spoke as if God's rich provision was nonexistent. He painted God as a wealthy father who dressed his children in rags and fed them mere crumbs. "Satan suggests that God is essentially prohibitive," explains James Montgomery Boice, "that he is not good, that he does not wish the very best of all worlds for his creatures."[9]

The moment Eve began to countenance such a misperception, the serpent went in for the kill. All subtlety was thrown to the wind. His indirect questioning and twisting of God's word gave way to outright, blatant denial of it. God had clearly set forth the death penalty as the consequence for eating of the tree of the knowledge of good and evil, but Satan contended, "You will not surely die" (Gen. 3:4). In other words, "God is a liar. His warning is simply not true. It is an empty threat." And like every skillful politician, Satan had his reasons why his opponent was not to be trusted: "For God knows that in the day you eat of it your eyes will be opened, and you will be like God, knowing good and evil" (v. 5). God, according to Satan, was an

---

9. James Montgomery Boice, *Genesis: An Expositional Commentary* (Grand Rapids: Baker Books, 2006), 1:165.

unloving, egotistical deceiver who did not have His creatures' best interest in mind.

The serpent understood something we are quick to overlook— a twisted view of God leads to a twisted view of self. The first step away from humility is a misperception of the divine. When we stop perceiving God as He truly is, we lose the ability to view ourselves as we truly are.

The Anatomy of the First Sin

Tragically, through the serpent's deceit, Eve embraced an idolatrous distortion of her fatherly Creator. We see this beginning to happen in Eve's reply to Satan's first question concerning God's restrictions. She responded in denial: "We may eat the fruit of the trees of the garden" (Gen. 3:2). So far so good, but Eve didn't stop there. She proceeded with further explanation: "but of the fruit of the tree which is in the midst of the garden, God has said, 'You shall not eat it, *nor shall you touch it*, lest you die'" (v. 3). Satan's ears were surely tickled with delight at hearing the words "nor shall you touch it." What was Eve doing? She was adding to God's prohibition. By doing so, she evidenced that she was beginning to perceive God as heavy-handed and stingy, and she was beginning to lose her innate fear of Him.

We often think that the fall into sin occurred when our first parents sunk their teeth into the forbidden fruit, but that is actually not the case. The fall began not when Adam and Eve embraced the serpent's words as true, but when they opened their minds to the possibility that his words might be true. When the serpent came with his God-distorting temptations, they should have stomped on his head by faith. God had called our first parents to guard His temple-garden as priests. But rather than purging the unholy one from the holy place, they welcomed his company and pondered his words. They weighed the potential soundness of his argument in the light of the tree's appearance (Gen. 3:6). And here is what we must understand—by opening their minds to the possible veracity of the serpent's speech, they put the serpent's word on the same level as God's word, only then to take up the gavel as judge. No longer was

God the sovereign Judge; Eve was. She assumed the prerogative to examine the evidence and to decide accordingly whether it was reasonable to believe and submit to her Creator. To put it simply, she cast off an all-controlling sense of her creatureliness. The autonomous self was enthroned as sovereign over God.

Is that clear to you? The chief problem was not an outward act of rebellion. Yes, eating the fruit was a gross, God-defying action. But before there was ever the external eating, there was first an internal disposition of haughtiness and self-exaltation. There was a rejection of the Creator-creature relationship in every faculty of the soul. Geerhardus Vos explains,

1. The manifestation of this fall was in the consciousness; there man recognizes himself as no longer living from God and for God.

2. The manifestation of this fall is in the alignment of the will of man. He no longer makes himself subject to God but seeks to be *like* God, above all not *less* than God.

3. The manifestation is in the emotional life of man. That he looks with lust and desire at the fruit that was forbidden by God shows how his emotion, too, functions in a wrong way, that it is no longer an enjoying of things in God but a godless losing of himself in things outside God.[10]

In their minds, wills, and affections, Adam and Eve had cast off the downward disposition of a Godward self-perception. They had rejected their Creator, thereby rejecting their own createdness. They became proud. And at the moment when the self was exalted above God, it was inevitable that they would take the fruit: "So when the woman saw that the tree was good for food, that it was pleasant to the eyes, and a tree desirable to make one wise, she took of its fruit and ate. She also gave to her husband with her, and he ate" (Gen. 3:6).

---

10. Vos, *Reformed Dogmatics*, 2:52.

The Anatomy of Our Sin

This was not the rebellion of an isolated couple or a mere individual. Through the covenant of works, Adam was functioning as the representative head of the entire human race. When he fell, we fell in him. When he failed to live in humble submission to his Creator, he plunged all of us into pride, for "through one man sin entered the world, and death through sin, and thus death spread to all men, because all sinned" in Adam (Rom. 5:12).[11] This creaturely conspiracy in God's garden-temple is the reason why all of us are conceived in sin (Ps. 51:5).

Every one of our personal sins shares the same anatomy as the first sin. According to Cornelius Van Til, the essence of all sin lies here—"Men virtually assume or presuppose that they are non-created."[12] Before anyone murders or commits adultery or lies or steals or takes God's name in vain, they first assume they are not creatures. Our external acts of rebellion are the ruinous result of our refusal to live in willful dependence on and subjection to our Creator. We deceive ourselves into believing that we are the lords of our own existence, that we are free to do as we please, and that we know better than our Creator.

Our nation celebrates the slaughter of millions of babies in the womb every year. A holocaust is happening in our backyard, and it is not without rationale. What would lead our culture to revel in such a grotesque violation of the sixth commandment? A woman's right to choose. Every woman, we are told, ought to be free to do with her body what she wants. The unargued assumption is that she is sovereign. She is not accountable to an absolutely authoritative Creator. God appears to be completely eradicated from the picture. The sixth commandment may come under consideration, but at the end of the day woman is lord and God's law is judged by the

---

11. For a thorough and insightful exposition of this text, see John Murray, *The Imputation of Adam's Sin* (Grand Rapids: Eerdmans, 1959).

12. As quoted in Greg L. Bahnsen, *Van Til's Apologetic: Readings and Analysis* (Phillipsburg, N.J.: P&R, 1998), 109.

sovereign self to be overly restrictive. Before she ever steps foot into Planned Parenthood, that mother must first reject her createdness, asserting the right to absolute, unqualified freedom. The blood on her hands from the murder of her own child does not arise out of thin air. It proceeds from pride.

Pride, the haughty disposition of an idolatrous self-perception, is the root of all sin. Think of the pornography endemic in the modern church. Millions of professing Christians regularly visit websites devoted to the sexually explicit. Are they simply unaware of God's hatred of these sex-distorting, woman-abusing, man-destroying, love-usurping images? No, that young man knows full well God's opposition to porn. He knows the seventh commandment, and he is likely familiar with Jesus's spiritual application of it (Matt. 5:27–28). He understands that those who fail to put their sexual lusts to death will die eternally (Matt. 5:29–30; 1 Cor. 6:9–10; Eph. 5:5–6), and he recognizes that a person cannot hold the fire of adultery to his chest without being burned alive (Prov. 6:27). But in the moment of temptation, he exalts himself as judge over God and His word. His twisted reasoning goes something like this: "God has said the way of the adulterous woman is the way of death, but I think there is life to be found here. Perhaps God is being overly restrictive. Perhaps He is a killjoy. Perhaps He is holding out on me. Perhaps He does not want to give me the best of all worlds. God has said the pleasure of porn will never satisfy my soul, but I know better than God. Besides, He will forgive me anyway." This is the arrogant disposition that leads him to willfully click on images he knows will defile and destroy him. He has disposed of his creatureliness and judged his Creator to be a dismal despot not worthy of allegiance. He has lost the downward disposition of a Godward self-perception.

Pride and the Death of Love

Do you see how pride is love's demise? The haughtiness undergirding abortion leads a mother to devalue the life of her child for the sake of preserving her own personal comfort. The haughtiness undergirding pornography leads a man to depersonalize women as objects to be used at will for his own sexual gratification. Exalting self leads to dehumanizing others.

All this was true of Adam and Eve's prideful rebellion. When confronted by God after partaking of the forbidden fruit, they ought to have owned their sin and repented. Adam should have confessed his failure to lead and protect his wife. But instead he blamed his wife. Then Eve blamed the serpent (Gen. 3:12–13). Our first parents had become consumed with themselves, viewing each other as the means of their own self-preservation and self-justification. When the downward disposition of humility is lost, the outward disposition of love goes with it. Our sin, in whatever form it might take, is always the death of true love.

CHAPTER 5

Delusional Sinners

At the time of the interview, Stefonknee Wolscht was a fifty-two-year-old biological male. Married for twenty-three years with seven children, Wolscht shared about his decision to leave his family behind. What led him to such a devastating act was an inner conviction that he actually isn't a male in his early fifties. According to his own testimony, Wolscht believes he is a six-year-old girl.[1] And he has decided to stop pretending otherwise. Though he still drinks coffee and drives a car, Wolscht dresses and plays like a first-grade female. He has even found a family to adopt him as their so-called daughter.

You cannot read the article about him without being overwhelmed by the irrationality of it all. The opening sentence reads, "A transgender father-of-seven in Canada has left her family to start living as a six-year-old girl." How can a father be referred to with the pronoun *her*? How can a six-year-old be the father of children in their teens? For Wolscht, along with his fellow sexual revolutionaries, "psychology trumps biology"[2]—but only when it is convenient.

---

1. Hannah Al-Othman, "Transgender Father Stefonknee Wolscht Leaves Family to Live as a Six-Year-Old Girl," *Evening Standard*, December 22, 2015, https://www.standard.co.uk/news/world/transgender-father-stefonknee-wolscht-leaves-family-to-live-as-a-sixyearold-girl-a3142551.html.

2. Carl R. Trueman, *The Rise and Triumph of the Modern Self: Cultural Amnesia, Expressive Individualism, and the Road to Sexual Revolution* (Wheaton, Ill.: Crossway, 2020), 369.

For though it is illegal for six-year-olds to operate motor vehicles in Canada, Stefonknee still drives his car.

Wolscht is living in a self-constructed delusion. His birth certificate says he is a male, but he has decided he is actually female. His driver's license says he is in his fifties, but he has concluded he is a six-year-old. "It's liberated me from the hurt," he told his interviewer, "because if I'm six years old I don't have to think about adult stuff." In other words, if Wolscht can convince himself that he is a child, he won't have to face up to the difficulties of adulthood. He is an adult, but he would rather not live in that reality. So he has created his own reality, which is actually anti-reality.

The story of Stefonknee Wolscht is no laughing matter. It is a distressing and stark picture of pride. Wolscht has enthroned the self as the sovereign definer of his person and purpose. His denial of God has led him to construct an unreality of the most disturbing kind. But lest we miss the lesson of this story, Wolscht, the fifty-two-year-old man living as a six-year-old girl, is actually a picture of all of us in our sin. Sure, our pride might not manifest itself in the outright denial of our biological makeup, but our sin leads us to live in no less delusive state.

All of us construct idolatrous self-perceptions that are nothing short of insane. As we saw in the last chapter, pride is the denial of who we are at the core of our beings. It is anti-reality. According to Charles Bridges, pride "contends for supremacy" with God.[3] The ultimate question is always, Who is supreme? In our sin, we assert the self as supreme. We attempt to "ungod" God and deify self, living as if we are the supreme creator. Wolscht's story ought to disturb you, but even more disturbing is that this man's anti-God, self-contrived world is simply the unrestrained outworking of the arrogance that reigns in every fallen child of Adam. In our fallen condition, we all live in a self-chosen delusion.

As we pursue a controlling sense of our own personal corruption, we turn to examine the illusory nature of sin. Our pride is insane,

---

3. As quoted in Mahaney, *Humility: True Greatness*, 31.

and few passages chronicle the utter irrationality of it like Romans 1:18–32. Paul wants us to see that in our rebellion we have lost our minds. Pride is the outright denial of the most basic truths of reality. It is a fundamental rejection of the Creator-creature relationship.

Denying the Inescapable Knowledge of Our Creator

The apostle begins by setting the Creator before us as a wrathful Judge who is angry with His image-bearing creatures. His wrath is on them because they "suppress the truth in unrighteousness" (Rom. 1:18). The act of *suppressing* literally means "to hold something down" or "to keep something under." Sinful people are experts at keeping the truth from rising to the surface.

When I was growing up, one of the popular arcade games was Whac-A-Mole. It consisted of a large, colorful machine with a bunch of metal mole heads that would randomly pop up. With a large, padded hammer, you were supposed to hit the moles back into the machine as fast as you could. I've sometimes wondered why the game was so enjoyable. Was it due to our intrinsic hatred of moles, or our enjoyment of smashing things with hammers? Probably both. It may be a stretch, but the theologian in me wonders if the reason I enjoyed Whac-A-Mole was because it resonates with me as a sinner. It serves as a parable of my pride. Whenever and wherever the truth rears its head, I am always laboring to smack it back into the ground as fast as I can. I must keep the truth from rising to the surface at all costs. That is what it means to suppress. We all are like sugar-intoxicated children frantically whacking mole heads back into the ground.

The truth that we suppress is not in the abstract. It is truth about God: "What may be known of God is manifest in them, for God has shown it to them. For since the creation of the world His invisible attributes are clearly seen, being understood by the things that are made, even His eternal power and Godhead, so that they are without excuse" (Rom. 1:19–20). It is God's self-revelation in creation that we labor so hard to keep underground. We call this *general revelation*. Consider four characteristics of this knowledge of God:

1. It is clear. This knowledge is "manifest" to us. In fact, it is so unavoidably obvious that all of us have "clearly seen" it.

2. It is divine. This knowledge is clear to us because "God has shown it" to us. God is disclosing truth about Himself, and as God, He makes sure His truth gets through.

3. It is specific. This is not knowledge of a vague deity, but the knowledge of the one, true, and living God. He is displaying to us "His invisible attributes...even His eternal power and Godhead."

4. It is everywhere. This knowledge is revealed "since the creation of the world" in "the things that are made." No time, place, or person has ever existed without the Creator's self-revelation.

The atheistic philosopher Bertrand Russell was once asked what he would tell God on judgment day if it turned out that God did indeed exist: "Not enough evidence! Not enough evidence!"[4] But the Scriptures tell us otherwise. The evidence is so clear, so pervasive, and so all-embracing that we "are without excuse" if we reject it (Rom. 1:20).

Given this, we would expect God's image-bearing creatures to receptively worship their glorious Creator for His wisdom, power, and dominion revealed in the created order. But in our sin, we do just the opposite. Confronted by the truth of God on every side, we whack it down. We know God, but we live as though we don't (Rom. 1:21). We know the truth, but we exchange it for a lie (v. 25). We want a reality without God, and we are willing to live in a delusion in our attempt to get it.

This delusion becomes even more striking when we remember that humans are image of God. The psalmist's praise is true—"The heavens declare the glory of God; and the firmament shows His handiwork" (Ps. 19:1). But the vast heavens are nothing compared to humankind. You and I are the clearest revelation of God's glory in all

---

4. As quoted in K. Scott Oliphint, *Covenantal Apologetics: Principles and Practice in Defense of Our Faith* (Wheaton, Ill.: Crossway, 2013), 114.

creation. Our spiritual, relational, vocational, and rational existence reflect God like no animal or inanimate object can. You might close your eyes to the glory revealed all around you, but you cannot escape the glory that is stamped on you as the apex of God's revelation in nature. Within and without, at all times and in all places, God is actively making known "all the divine perfections" to you.[5]

Everywhere the glory of your Creator is popping up its head. But we want a reality without His glory in which we can reign supreme. We want to be lord and not have to answer to and depend on our sovereign Creator-King. So we devote our lives to denying what we actually know to be true.

Denying the Incomparable Worth of Our Creator

Our denial of the knowledge of God's glory is idolatrous. We were created to worship. You and I will always worship someone or something. If we reject the One who alone is worthy of our worship, we will turn to idols. Though we know God through His clear revelation, in our depravity we do "not glorify Him as God" (Rom. 1:21). Honor is the most reasonable response of image-bearing creatures to their Creator, but in our fallen condition we refuse to give it. We will not give God glory. We will not praise Him as our chief delight. We will not thank Him as the One who supplies to us all things.

Van Til once described sinful people as a little girl sitting in the lap of her loving father. With a scowl on her face, the daughter lifts her hand and angrily slaps her father across the face. Consider Van Til's point. For this girl to slap her dad necessitates her sitting in his lap and depending on his support. That is you in your sin— surrounded by God and entirely dependent on Him even as you perpetually slap Him across the face. It is madness—and it is madness in which all sinners indulge.

In Adam we refuse to honor and thank God, and instead we render honor and thanks to created things: "Professing to be wise, they

---

5. Charles Hodge, *Commentary on the Epistle to the Romans* (Grand Rapids: Eerdmans, 1994), 37.

became fools, and changed the glory of the incorruptible God into an image made like corruptible man—and birds and four-footed animals and creeping things" (Rom. 1:22–23). Pride is an exchange. We exchange our Creator's incomparable worth for the creature's derivative worth.

Imagine that when I get home tonight, I find myself greeted by a rambunctious and adorable puppy. I have wanted a puppy for some time, and my wife decided to surprise me with a gift. I immediately name him Luther and am so taken up with him that I don't even bother to thank my wife. As the days pass, I become infatuated with Luther. I spend all my free time with him. I take him out on doggy dates. I spend my life's savings on making sure he has the latest doggy toys and clothes. And I even ask my wife to start sleeping on the couch so that Luther can sleep next to me. You would say I had lost my mind! And you would be right. The gift (a puppy) should have increased my love and devotion to the giver (my wife), but instead the gift became the means by which I deserted and despised the giver. That is what we do in our sin—we exalt the gifts above the giver; we delight in the creature above the Creator. And in case you think this is something only unbelievers do, that is not the case. To whatever extent pride clings to us after conversion, Christians do the same. Every sin you and I commit is rooted in this arrogant exchange.

Our idolatry might not be as recognizable as first-century Gentiles bowing before statues of gold and silver. But our idolatry is just as real and just as delusional. For what do we exchange God's glory? Where do we seek our joy and satisfaction? In material prosperity, political power, career success, sexual pleasure, physical health, celebrity icons, and the like. These are the idols before which sophisticated twenty-first-century sinners bow.

Take gluttony, for example, which Jerry Bridges terms a "respectable sin."[6] Overindulgence in food and drink is culturally acceptable, even within the church. We make jokes about it—and we expect it. Phrases like "the freshman fifteen" are commonplace and uttered

---

6. See Jerry Bridges, *Respectable Sins* (Colorado Springs: NavPress, 2007).

without the slightest ethical concern. But gluttony is the result of the same truth-suppressing, God-denying pride as sexual immorality or murder. I know because I personally struggle with overindulging in food. After a stressful meeting or a tiring day, my native tendency is to turn to the refrigerator. To be clear, food is a good gift from God to be enjoyed. The problem is not the dark chocolate brownie and Brazilian dark roast; the problem is my dark heart. I'm looking to a created thing to satisfy my longings and needs as only my Creator can. Food has become an idol, and so I eat and eat and eat, believing that each bite will swallow up my sorrow and provide lasting joy. But it is a delusion. And anyone who struggles with gluttony knows it. Food cannot satisfy the deep longings of the soul. But in our sinful insanity, we keep going back to it as if it will. And when we do, we reject the offer of infinite satisfaction in Christ. Here is the madness of gluttony—I exchange the eternal pleasure of Christ for the passing pleasure of chocolate. That is not something to joke about or to treat lightly. That is an evil deserving nothing less than the wrath of God.

Denying the Irreversible Design of Our Creator

Paul tells us that our prideful embrace of an idolatrous delusion has resulted in "the wrath of God [being] revealed from heaven" (Rom. 1:18). Yes, there is a future day of wrath (2:5). But even now, in the present, the wrath of God is being publicly displayed toward sinful humanity. The thought of divine wrath revealed from heaven probably conjures up images of celestial lightning bolts striking people dead. But the revelation of God's righteous fury is more commonplace than we might imagine. Even when there is not a cloud in the sky and the sun is beaming on us, God's wrath is revealed in God giving people over to their self-chosen delusion: "Therefore God also gave them up to uncleanness, in the lusts of their hearts, to dishonor their bodies among themselves" (Rom. 1:24; cf. 2 Thess. 2:11).

The words "God also gave them up" are some of the most terrifying in the whole Bible. God is lifting His gracious restraint. In His wrath He is saying, "You have defied Me and gone your own way, and in My judgment, I am not coming after you. I'm leaving you to your own illusory devices. I'm handing you over to your sin in order that you might self-destruct." God does this because they "exchanged the truth of God for the lie, and worshiped and served the creature rather than the Creator, who is blessed forever" (Rom. 1:25). It is the haughty, God-denying disposition of an idolatrous self-perception that has warranted the wrath of God.

The apostle zeros in on a specific example of God giving prideful humanity over to their sin. It is a most sobering example given our present cultural moment: "For this reason God gave them up to vile passions. For even their women exchanged the natural use for what is against nature. Likewise also the men, leaving the natural use of the woman, burned in their lust for one another, men with men committing what is shameful, and receiving in themselves the penalty of their error which was due" (Rom. 1:26–27). The language is unavoidably clear. One way God's wrath is being revealed is in men and women being given over to homosexual passions. It is hard to imagine a more offensive statement in our secular society, but there is a good reason why Paul draws on homosexuality as the primary example of sinful desire. He has been alluding to Genesis 1–2 throughout these verses in an attempt to help us to see that our pride is essentially a rejection of the created order.[7] Our idolatry "seeks fundamentally to change, to perversely reverse, the natural, created order of the world."[8] And can you think of a starker example of that than men having sexual relations with men and women having sexual relations with women? Such relations, to use the apostle's words, are "against nature." They are simply not ordered according to God's good design of the sexual union enjoyed by a husband and wife.

A couple of months ago, the city in which I pastor hosted what they termed a gay pride festival. Though the sexual revolutionaries

---

7. See Kevin DeYoung, *What Does the Bible Really Teach about Homosexuality?* (Wheaton, Ill.: Crossway, 2015), 52–55.

8. K. Scott Oliphint, "The Irrationality of Unbelief: An Exegetical Study," in *Revelation and Reason: New Essays in Reformed Apologetics*, ed. K. Scott Oliphint and Lane G. Tipton (Phillipsburg, N.J.: P&R, 2007), 71.

are clearly not operating with a biblical definition of pride, they are, in God's wisdom, calling their sin what it is. The celebration of homosexuality is always the celebration of the autonomous self. No creatures are ever actually laws unto themselves, but pride is the willful delusion that we are. And homosexuality, according to the Scriptures, is one clear manifestation of it.

The sexual revolution that is swiftly conquering the West and becoming more extreme by the hour is a revelation of God's righteous judgment as He gives sinners over to their confused, distorted, and delusive condition. This is cause not for scoffing, but for getting low before God. To read of the LGBTQ agenda in the morning newspaper is to be given a picture of our own hearts by nature. Homosexuality and transgenderism are striking pictures of the unnaturalness of every sin. Sin is anti-reality, denying the Designer and His design of the universe. And that arrogant denial manifests itself in a nearly unending variety of ways in our hearts and lives (see Rom. 1:29–31).

Denying the Incorruptible Judgment of Our Creator

Pride is willful self-deception. Though we know God, we live as though we do not. Though we know He alone is worthy of worship, we live as though He is not. Though we recognize God has ordered the world in a particular way, we live as though He has not. Our attempt to ungod the Creator has resulted in insanity of the highest sort. Pride is the denial of reality, and it reaches not only to the past and present but to the future.

Notice how Paul draws his description of our sinful condition to a close: "who, knowing the righteous judgment of God, that those who practice such things are deserving of death, not only do the same but also approve of those who practice them" (Rom. 1:32). As God's image, we possess an inescapable awareness not only that we have been created but also that we are morally accountable to our Creator. This is because, though severely marred by the fall, we have the remains of God's law written on our hearts (2:14–15). Fallen people possess a conscience that plagues them with guilt. We know we are sinful, and we know that our sin warrants the sword of God's judgment. The reasonable response to such knowledge is to admit our folly and seek mercy from the hand of God. But that is not what we do. Instead, we suppress the knowledge of this future reality.

The truth is that there is no pleasure in sin when you know it warrants death and hell. It is like trying to enjoy a mouth-watering steak when you know it has been slathered in deadly poison. In order to enjoy those few bites of red meat, you have to deny the poisonous reality. Do you reject what you know to be true about yourself and your future simply because you find sin enjoyable, despite its being plastered with warning labels? Or do you celebrate the sin of others because it comforts and confirms you in your own delusional condition? The sad reality is that this is the world in which we live. Is that not the great reason pride is paraded in our streets?

Brought Low by Our Delusive Depravity

Haughtiness cannot thrive in the heart that has reckoned with the insanity of sin. Our arrogance is evidence that we don't understand our delusive depravity. It is not necessarily that we don't understand Romans 1 or the biblical doctrine of sin, but our unspoken hermeneutic is that passages like this are pictures of people out there, not of us.

Perhaps you had the great privilege of growing up in a Christian home. Perhaps in God's kindness you can never remember a time when you were not trusting in Jesus. What a tremendous blessing! But that blessing is accompanied with a potential danger—failing to grasp the sinfulness of *your* sin. Romans 1 is your self-portrait apart from God's grace. Take a good look at what you are by nature in Adam: "undiscerning, untrustworthy, unloving, unforgiving, unmerciful" (v. 31).

Is this not grounds for the downward disposition of humility? Left to our own devices, all of us choose to live in the fiction of uncreatedness. We are fools in Adam. By nature we are really no different from Stefonknee Wolscht, constructing an anti-reality of self-destructive autonomy. In fact, we so delude ourselves in our hatred of God that nothing in the created order can bring us to our senses. We are natively fit for a spiritual insane asylum. Oh, for a controlling sense of our folly in Adam! Oh, how we need God's word to cut us deep at this point! Every sin you and I commit is undergirded by the delusion of pride. Whether gossip or gluttony, adultery or anger, laziness or lukewarmness, our sin, even as Christians, is the result of an idolatrous self-perception. Such a self-perception can only live and thrive when God is removed from the picture. Is this not cause for weeping, for getting out sackcloth and throwing dust on our heads? But the reality is that all of us possess a deluded perspective of our delusive depravity. That is why our eyes don't weep and our hearts don't groan. We are deceived about our deception. And only God by His word and Spirit can cause us to see our sin with increasing clarity. Only He can work in us the profound lowliness elicited by the controlling sense of our corruption.

CHAPTER 6

Hopeless Sinners

Despair is the psychological state of hopelessness. We despair when we find ourselves in a miserable condition without the slightest expectation of deliverance. A person cannot live long without hope. The cancer patient willingly undergoes the misery of chemotherapy from the conviction of potential healing. The soldier willingly risks everything in battle from the conviction of potential victory. But when such grounds for hope are lost, there is no reason to continue. Hope is a powerful force, apart from which we sink into the pit of despondency and death.

Tragically, every fallen son of Adam is void of sincere and solid hope. In our sin, we are without hope and without God (Eph. 2:12). Hopeless despair is our reality, but in our pride, we choose anti-reality. No one can live without hope, so we delude ourselves with idolatrous hopes. We convince ourselves that things are not as bad as they seem and that we are not as bad as we seem. We do everything in our power to avoid the truth of our hopeless condition.

A controlling sense of our native corruption would be incomplete without considering our utter inability to undo our woeful condition. The downward disposition of humility is founded on the fact that we are entirely helpless to free ourselves from our corruption and its consequences. Left to ourselves, there is not the slightest chance of deliverance. We are hopelessly sinful.

No Escape from Sin's Penalty

Beatrix Potter's classic *Tale of Peter Rabbit* is the story of a mischievous young rabbit named Peter who is caught red-handed stealing vegetables from the mean old Mr. McGregor. Peter trespasses, entering into McGregor's garden without permission and taking what does not belong to him. And he almost gets put into Mrs. McGregor's pie for it! Like Peter Rabbit, we have gone places we ought not to and taken things that do not belong to us. But unlike Peter, who escaped the dreaded butcher's knife of Mrs. McGregor, we can run but we cannot hide. That is because we have stolen not from a fellow creature, but ultimately from our Creator.

Guilt in the Garden

In rich generosity God had given our first parents all the trees of the garden to enjoy except one. A singular tree was off-limits. And God's butcher knife was sharpened and ready for any who would trespass (Gen. 2:17). He had warned Adam and Eve that the slightest infringement of His restriction would result in guilt, condemnation, and ultimately death. Trespassing the Creator's law was a legal violation of the highest order, warranting an eternal death sentence.

In the bliss of their original condition, Adam and Eve had never known guilt or shame (Gen. 2:25). They were strangers to guilt because they had never broken the law written on their hearts. They were strangers to shame because they had no imperfections to hide. But all of that changed the moment they rose up in autonomous revolt. That first trespass opened the floodgates of guilt and shame, and for the first time, Adam and Eve sensed the need to hide. Resorting to their own ingenuity, they quickly patched together coverings of leaves (3:7). And then we read one of the most tragic statements ever uttered: "And they heard the sound of the LORD God walking in the garden in the cool of the day, and Adam and his wife hid themselves from the presence of the LORD God among the trees of the garden" (v. 8). As image of God, Adam and Eve were created for intimate communion with their fatherly Creator. They had always relished in His presence. The controlling impulse of their souls was incessantly *toward* their Creator, not *away from* Him. But now as the Original approaches, the image is running scared. Now as the Creator draws near, the creature is hiding in terror. Adam and Eve had trespassed. "They had lost the ethical glory of God-likeness," writes Meredith Kline, "which is the prerequisite to stand as priest before the Face of God and reflect the Glory of God."[1] They were guilty and knew they were fit for the divine butcher block, so they sought a place of refuge. But when you are hiding from the Creator, the only hiding place left is the creation. They hid behind leaves, looking to the work of their own hands. They hid behind trees, using the Creator's gifts to evade the Creator Himself. They were desperate to avoid the holy eyes of God. Despite their best attempts, however, there was no escape. No work of their hands could cover their guilt. Nothing in the created order could deliver. The Creator will not be trifled with, nor will He leave trespasses unpunished. He drew near to Adam and Eve in judgment.

Guilt in Us

Like our first parents, all of us are trespassers. "For all have sinned and fall short of the glory of God" (Rom. 3:23). We have exchanged our Creator's infinite glory for finite creaturely idols. We are guilty before a holy God, and there is no escaping sin's penalty. We can't wash our sin-stained souls or erase our criminal records. We can run, but we can't hide. And we don't need God to tell us this. We know it intuitively. Even the most seared conscience cannot avoid being alarmed at times by a sense of guilt and shame.

There I sat in the middle school cafeteria, a sixth grader with a filthy mind and a foul mouth. I wanted to be accepted and esteemed by my peers. And I thought blasphemy was the way to gain their favor. With a bite of cheeseburger between my teeth, I vilified the name of God, committing blasphemy of the most monstrous sort. But my God-hating words did not have the effect on my buddies that I imagined they would. "You are going to go to hell, man," replied

---

1. Kline, *Kingdom Prologue*, 130.

my friend with a look of genuine concern. His words struck a force-
ful blow. For a moment, I saw my guilt. I recognized that I deserved
to be in Mrs. McGregor's pie. I trembled at God's wrath and sensed
the need to hide. My image-bearing conscience was sounding the
alarm: *Guilty! Guilty! Guilty!* But that moment passed, and within
a few hours I had deluded myself into believing I was just fine. Like
every sinner, I was (and continue to be) a professional when it came
to self-justification.

The piercing words of Samuel Davies ring true of every one of
us in our pride:

> The knowledge of yourselves, the knowledge of disagreeable
> duties, the discovery of your sin and danger, of your miser-
> able condition as under the condemnation of the divine law,
> this kind of self-knowledge you carefully shun; and, when it
> irresistibly flashes upon you, you endeavor to shut up all the
> avenues of your mind, through which it might break upon you,
> and you avoid those means of conviction from which it pro-
> ceeds.... When the ill-boding surmise rises within, "All is not
> well: I am not prepared for the eternal world: if I should die in
> this condition, I am undone for ever"; I say, when conscience
> thus whispers your doom, it may make you sad and pensive
> for a minute or two, but you soon forget it: you designedly
> labour to cast it out of your thoughts and to recover your for-
> mer negligent serenity. The light of conviction is a painful glare
> to a guilty eye: and you wrap yourselves up in darkness, lest it
> should break in upon you.[2]

What is every false religion but sinful creatures' futile attempt to
hide from their just Creator, pridefully wrapping themselves in darkness and attempting to cover over their guilt by the works of their
hands? False religions are just fig leaves—creatures in a desperate
attempt to deliver themselves from their inescapable condemnation. Even atheism is an attempt at self-salvation. Atheists suppress

---

2. Samuel Davies, "The Rejection of Gospel-Light the Condemnation of
Men," in *Sermons of the Rev. Samuel Davies* (Morgan, Pa.: Soli Deo Gloria,
1995), 3:39–40.

their guilty conscience by suppressing the truth of their Creator altogether. If they can wipe out the Judge of all the earth, they can wipe out the death sentence written on their foreheads. But no person can wipe out his or her Creator. Despite their best attempts, people cannot remove the infinite guilt they have brought on themselves by sin.

Guilt to the Infinite Degree

Pride speaks peace where there is no peace, but humility reckons with the guilt of sin. This downward disposition of soul leads corrupt creatures to see themselves as hopelessly condemned to death. For, as Thomas Boston argues, sinful people must do two things to deliver themselves from the guilt of sin. First, they must perfectly keep the commands of God with all of their heart. Second, they must make perfect satisfaction for the sins they have already committed.[3] With regard to the second, he writes, "It may be you have changed your course of life, or are now resolved to do it, and to set about keeping the commands of God: but what have you done, or what will you do, with the old debt? Your obedience to God, though it were perfect, is a debt due to him for the time wherein it is performed, and can no more satisfy for former sins, than a tenant's paying the current year's rent can satisfy the landlord for all arrears [outstanding payments due]."[4] Boston is speaking hypothetically. Corrupt creatures like us can never perfectly obey God. But even if from this moment forward we did, it could not erase the guilt and punishment incurred from past sins. Perfect obedience is paying the day's bills. It is simply what we owe to God as creatures. Today's obedience has no ability to pay yesterday's debt. "Let me now ask you," Boston continues, "are you able to satisfy the justice of God? Can you pay your own debt? Surely not: for, as He is the infinite God, whom you have offended, the punishment, being suited to the quality of the offence,

---

3. Thomas Boston, *Human Nature in Its Fourfold State: Of Primitive Integrity, Entire Depravity, Begun Recovery, and Consummate Happiness or Misery* (Edinburgh: Banner of Truth, 1964), 183–89.

4. Boston, *Human Nature in Its Fourfold State*, 187.

must be infinite. But your punishment, or sufferings for sin, cannot be infinite in value, for you are a finite creature: therefore, they must be infinite in duration or continuance; that is, they must be eternal."[5]

You and I have incurred a debt of infinite proportions. We have no ability to right our wrongs or to make satisfaction for our sins. And God, being perfectly just, cannot push our sins under the rug, pretending they don't exist. The just penalty for our trespasses is eternal death, for sin, as we have seen, is defying the infinitely glorious God. One single sin in our thoughts, desires, words, or actions is enough to warrant everlasting damnation. And we are utterly hopeless to deliver ourselves from it.

Do you believe that—that it is not enough to simply clean up your act and do better, that there is no way for you to remove the stain of your sin? That left to yourself you are locked in a prison of guilt and shame from which you cannot save yourself? That God cannot turn a blind eye to your rebellion without denying Himself? None of us possess the ability to escape our holy Creator's pronouncement of eternal condemnation. The downward disposition of humility embraces this. The lowly in spirit confess, "I am hopelessly guilty in and of myself!" They agree with their Creator-Judge, pronouncing their own self-condemnation.

No Escape from Sin's Power

The sin that condemns us is the sin that enslaves us. The great pastor-theologian Augustine knew what it was to be bound in the shackles of sin. Steeped in pagan philosophy and striving after worldly accolades, Augustine was on a desperate quest for meaning and satisfaction. While in Milan, he became strongly drawn to the biblical preaching of Bishop Ambrose. He listened with great interest, but he found himself unable to turn to the God whom Ambrose proclaimed. "Your beauty drew me to you," he confessed to the Lord, "but soon I was dragged away from you by my own weight and in dismay I plunged again into the things of this world...

---

5. Boston, *Human Nature in Its Fourfold State*, 187.

as though I had sensed the fragrance of the fare but was not yet able to eat it."[6] The specific sin that held him in bondage was sexual immorality: "I was still held firm in the bonds of woman's love."[7] For Augustine, his mistress's beauty was more alluring than the beauty of God. The fleeting pleasures of sex were more valuable than the everlasting pleasures of God. Augustine was proud. He exalted the creature above the Creator. He discovered that, despite his best efforts at reformation of life, he had no ability to break free from the mastery of his idolatrous lust. He was hopelessly enslaved to sin.

Not Able Not to Sin

What was true of Augustine is true of all of us by nature. We inherit not only the guilt of Adam's sin but also its pollution. Our condition in Adam is one of spiritual death—"dead in trespasses and sins" (Eph. 2:1). As corrupt creatures, we are not merely spiritually wounded or diseased. We are spiritually dead, and with that death comes inability.

Susan was a loving wife and mother of three, but she is so no more. A tragic accident on Saturday afternoon took her life. Susan is dead, and today is her funeral. As you stand in line to offer your condolences to her family, you watch as Susan's little girl quietly slips away from her father's side. She walks over to her mother's open casket, climbs up on a chair, and starts shaking the lifeless corpse inside. With tears streaming down her face, she cries, "Please, Mommy, wake up! Please don't leave me! Please come back!" The scene is devastating. Just last week, this little girl had fallen off her scooter, scraped up her elbow, and cried out for Susan. That cry reached Susan's ears, moving her to run to her daughter and scoop her up in her loving arms. But now the agonizing cries of her daughter have no ability to move her. Susan cannot hear. She cannot think. She cannot embrace her daughter. She cannot speak words of comfort to her. She is dead.

6. Augustine, *Confessions*, trans. R. S. Pine-Coffin (New York: Penguin, 1961), 152.

7. Augustine, *Confessions*, trans. Pine-Coffin, 158.

That is a picture of us in our sin—one of morbid inability. We have no ability to seek God or obey Him. We have no ability to believe God's word. Spiritually speaking, we are a corpse of decomposing flesh, and like Susan's lifeless body in the casket, we can do nothing to resuscitate ourselves:

> There is none righteous, no, not one;
> There is none who understands;
> There is none who seeks after God.
> They have all turned aside;
> They have together become unprofitable;
> There is none who does good, no, not one.
> (Rom. 3:10–12)

Because we are dead in sin, we are not able to do anything but sin.

But Isn't the Will Free?

Now maybe you are thinking, "But surely, I could do good if I wanted to. Surely I could seek God if I desired to. After all, I have free will!" No one is denying that if you truly wanted to, you could obey and follow God. The problem is that spiritually dead people never genuinely desire to do God's will for God's glory. In our sinful hearts, we hate God (Rom. 1:30). We possess a native hostility to God that makes it impossible for our wills to submit to Him. "Because of the bondage of sin by which the will is held bound," Calvin explains, "it cannot move toward good, much less apply itself thereto.… Nonetheless the will remains, with the most eager inclination disposed and hastening to sin. For man, when he gave himself over to this necessity, was not deprived of will, but of soundness of will."[8] Sinners still have the ability to will, but they have lost the ability to will soundly. Our wills do not make choices in a vacuum. Every choice we make is driven by our affections. We choose according to what we value and desire. And corrupt creatures never value and desire their Creator.

---

8. Calvin, *Institutes*, 2.3.5.

In South Korea live octopus is a delicacy, likened to filet mignon in America. Imagine my Korean friend has invited me over for authentic Korean cuisine, and he has decided to serve his best. He appears from the kitchen with a plate of live octopus, tentacles still squirming, and eagerly sets it before me. After a prolonged pause, I look at my friend and say with regret, "I'm sorry, but I cannot eat this." Is that the truth? Don't I have free will? Yes, in one sense my will is free to choose to eat or not to eat. But it is no exaggeration to state that I cannot eat it. Why not? Because my affections are completely opposed to such a notion. The thought of slurping down a live octopus disgusts me. Not only that, but I have heard stories of people choking to death on these slimy sea creatures, and I value my life. In fact, I value my life more than I value pleasing my friend. And so not only will I not eat it, but, given the present condition of my affections, I cannot eat it. The only way I could choose to eat is if my desire to please my friend was greater than my desire to avoid the disgusting and deadly slime. If ever I was so enslaved to the fear of man, then yes, I could choose to eat. But that just proves the point that we always choose according to our strongest desires and values. The will is governed by the affections.

Our problem in sin is not that we have no ability to will. It is that our wills are governed by affections that are relentlessly repulsed by God. You and I are free to do as we desire, but in our rebellious, prideful condition, we never genuinely desire God. To live in dependent submission to Him is more intolerable than swallowing a live octopus, so we will not come to God—indeed, we cannot. "So then, those who are in the flesh cannot please God" (Rom. 8:8).

Corrupt in Totality

This is our hopeless condition in sin. Try as we may, we have no ability to break free from sin's grip. Every faculty of our soul is in idolatrous bondage:

- Sinful lies govern our reason. Having rejected the fear of the Lord, we have lost true knowledge and wisdom.

- Sinful values govern our affections. Having rejected the Lord as our chief treasure, we exult in the creature.

- Sinful choices govern our will. Having rejected the Lord's authority over us, we go our own way.

Though dead, we are, in the words of R. C. Sproul, "diabolically alive."[9] The power of satanic pride holds the totality of our persons in its indomitable grip.

That doesn't mean we are as bad as we could possibly be. Because of God's gracious restraint, many of us appear well mannered and civilized in our sinful condition.[10] But while the outside might appear nicely polished, within we are a tomb of rotting, God-defying corruption (Matt. 23:27). We are spiritually dead. We wave to our neighbors, give to charities, and work respectable jobs, but in our hearts, all of us by nature are hell-worthy idolaters. Every one of our thoughts, words, and actions is shot through with serpentine arrogance. And we lack the ability to change that. This is you and me by nature—hopelessly corrupt in Adam.

Is There Any Hope for Me?

It is a Godward self-perception that results in the controlling sense of our hopeless condition in sin. When we see ourselves before God's unbounded glory, we recognize that our defiance of Him has incurred a debt of infinite proportions we can never repay. We are hopelessly condemned and subject to eternal death. When we see ourselves before the manifold perfections of God, we recognize that even our best deeds are wrath deserving and we cannot perform a single deed as we ought. We are hopelessly corrupt and bound fast in sin. What lowliness this God-entranced vision of the self ought to produce in us!

---

9. R. C. Sproul, *What Is Reformed Theology?: Understanding the Basics* (Grand Rapids: Baker Books, 1997), 129.

10. See John Murray, "Common Grace," in *Collected Writings of John Murray* (Edinburgh: Banner of Truth, 1977), 93–119.

Have you been mastered by your hopeless condition in Adam? Have you despaired of looking to yourself or anything in the created order to deliver you from sin's penalty and power? "The truth is," asserts William Plumer, "no man ever thought himself a greater sinner before God than he really was. Nor was any man ever more distressed at his sins than he had just cause to be."[11] None of us understands our plight in Adam as we ought. But the more forcefully this reality grips our souls, the lower our souls will descend. And descend they must because it is only humility that will enable us to turn away from our hopeless selves to the God of hope.

In 1907 a group of saints gathered in Pyongyang, Korea, for prayer. They were desperate for the advance of Christ's kingdom and began to seek God earnestly for it. One missionary described the meeting as "a mingling together of souls moved by an irresistible impulse of prayer."[12] As these believers called on the Lord, the Spirit descended in an extraordinary manner, and the result was nothing less than a controlling sense of corruption. "As prayer continued," recounted this missionary,

> a spirit of heaviness and sorrow for sin came down upon the audience. Over on one side, someone began to weep, and in a moment the whole audience was weeping. Man after man would rise, confess his sins, break down and weep, and then throw himself to the floor and beat the floor with his fists in perfect agony of conviction. My own cook tried to make a confession, broke down in the midst of it, and cried to me across the room: "Pastor, tell me, is there any hope for me, can I be forgiven?" and then threw himself to the floor and wept and wept, and almost screamed in agony.[13]

---

11. William Plumer, *The Grace of Christ* (Keyser, W. Va.: Odom, 1853), 20.
12. As quoted in Thomas Kidd, "The North Korean Revival of 1907," *Thomas Kidd* (blog), The Gospel Coalition, May 2, 2017, https://www.thegospel coalition.org/blogs/evangelical-history/the-north-korean-revival-of-1907/.
13. As quoted in Kidd, "North Korean Revival of 1907."

A Spirit-wrought conviction of sin will bring us low. It will cast us to the floor. Like Isaiah, we will be shattered into a million pieces in agonizing woe. But true humility does not stop there. God is not interested in giving us a controlling sense of our corruption merely to make us miserable. He strips us of our vain hopes so that we might cry out in desperation, "Tell me, is there any hope for me? Can I be forgiven? Can I be set free?" God brings us down so that we might look up. He decimates our creaturely confidence so that we might cast ourselves on Him. God humbles us not to destroy us, but to deliver us, for only when we are delivered from our prideful delusion will we see our need of a divine Deliverer. It is to that Deliverer we now turn.

PART 3

Evangelical Humility

evangelical: pertaining to the gospel or good news
We are represented, foreloved, and adopted believers.

CHAPTER 7

Represented Believers

The year was 1807. The city was London. The man was William Jay. He was a relatively new pastor, going to visit his spiritual mentor one final time. He stepped into the bedroom, where an eighty-two-year-old disabled and dying man lay, ready to drink in whatever wisdom he could. Who was the elderly man? John Newton, the English pastor best known for his hymn "Amazing Grace." We don't know all that was said in that hour, but young William jotted down one sentence from Newton's dying lips: "My memory is nearly gone, but I remember two things: that I am a great sinner and that Christ is a great Savior."[1]

By nature, all of us are hopelessly delusional sinners. With Newton, the humble grapple with their fallen condition in Adam. But more perceptive readers may be left wondering up to this point, "Where is Christ in all of this?" After all, the book's subtitle stresses that true humility is inseparably related to Him.

I am a minister of the gospel. I live on the gospel. I recognize that for great sinners like us, our only hope is a great Savior. It has been exceedingly difficult to refrain from speaking of the gospel to this point. "Woe is me if I do not preach the gospel!" (1 Cor. 9:16). But I am convinced that belief in the gospel is preceded by a sense

---

1. As quoted in Jonathan Aitken, *John Newton: From Disgrace to Amazing Grace* (Wheaton, Ill.: Crossway, 2007), 347.

of creatureliness and corruption. Apart from these truths, the gospel doesn't even make sense.[2] Our own creatureliness and corruption have been the focus until now, but they cannot be where we end, for postfall humility is always gospel humility.

God's Grace in God's Garden

Adam and Eve had risen up in autonomous revolt against God. They had denied their creatureliness, put God's word on the same level as Satan's, and judged their Creator to be a liar. With the divine death penalty ringing in their ears, they pridefully ate the forbidden fruit. As God drew near in holy judgment, our parents tried to cover themselves and hide. But no creature ingenuity could shelter them from their covenant Lord.

God's Gracious Initiative

The Lord pursued His rebellious image bearer with a question: "Where are you?" (Gen. 3:9). God did not ask this out of a deficiency of knowledge. He did not lack the precise geographical location of His creature. His question was aimed at bringing Adam to see and confess his ruinous condition.[3] In essence, God was saying, "You have always been drawn like a magnet to My presence, Adam. Never before have you been repelled by the sound of My approach. What has happened, My son?" God would not leave His image delusively hiding behind leaves and bark. He pursued Adam and Eve, piercing their hearts with convicting questions that exposed their sin (vv. 11–13). While the image was running scared, the Original drew near. He sought our first parents when they did not seek Him.

---

2. I am following John Calvin here: "First, as much in the fashioning of the universe as in the general teaching of Scripture the Lord shows himself to be simply the Creator. Then in the face of Christ he shows himself the Redeemer. Of the resulting twofold knowledge of God we shall now discuss the first aspect; the second will be dealt with in its proper place." *Institutes*, 1.2.1.

3. Waltke with Fredricks, *Genesis: A Commentary*, 92.

Through their Creator's pointed questions, Adam and Eve were given a controlling sense of their corruption. They were given a lesson in postfall humility. Contrary to expectation, however, this was not a wrathful humbling. God did not expose their guilt only to strike them dead with the sword of His justice. He exposed them in order to prepare them for His promise. The lips that brought conviction were about to bring consolation. But strangely, God's comfort came in the form of a curse. To the arrogant serpent, God declared,

> I will put enmity
> Between you and the woman,
> And between your seed and her Seed;
> He shall bruise your head,
> And you shall bruise His heel. (Gen. 3:15)[4]

Throughout the church's history, this curse has been rightly understood as the first gospel promise. The first preacher of grace was God Himself!

But how can the announcement of bitter hostility and bloody warfare be classified as the gospel? On the surface, that hardly seems like good news. If World War III were to break out tomorrow, we would not be filled with praise. War entails sacrifice, pain, trauma, and grave loss. So how is God's promise of continual warfare between the serpent and Eve good news?

This sworn enmity is joyful tidings only to those who grasp the nature of the fall into sin. Eve had sided with Satan. She had espoused the same haughty disposition and idolatrous self-perception that he possessed. In her pride she had formed an alliance with the serpent. But by this curse-filled promise, God was swearing, "Eve, this coalition between you and the serpent will not continue. You have sided with Satan, but in My sovereign grace, I am going to win you back to

---

4. This is actually the second part of God's curse on the serpent. In verse 14, God subjects the serpent to crawl on his belly in the dirt. God brings this haughty angel low, forcing him to eat the dust. It is a picture of military defeat (e.g., Micah 7:17) and of what will become of all those who remain under Satan's dominion. In God's time, all the haughty will be cut down.

Myself. You are Mine." This is pure grace. Eve had defied her Creator in satanic arrogance. She deserved death. But instead, her Creator drew near as Deliverer to free her from her servitude to Satan. And this salvation was not for Eve alone, but for all her spiritual children.[5] In God's rich grace, some of Eve's physical offspring would be delivered from satanic bondage. They would no longer be children of the devil, but children of God.

The divine *I* in the promise mustn't be overlooked. God declared, "*I* will put enmity." Neither Eve nor her husband would bring about this spiritual hostility. They were entirely powerless to free themselves from the penalty and power of their devilish pride. They were hopelessly condemned and corrupt. They were helplessly bound to the serpent. But God refused to leave them there. In His grace, He initiated their salvation. He pursued, He pierced, and He promised. And all that was left for Adam and Eve to do was believe.

God's Gracious Accomplishment
God's curse on the serpent would progress from a universal warfare embracing the entire human race to a specific conflict between Satan and one of Eve's descendants. God said of this One, "He shall bruise your head, and you shall bruise His heel" (Gen. 3:15). Within the broader enmity unfolding between these two seeds, one-to-one combat would ensue between Satan and a son of Eve.[6] Both parties would suffer in the conflict. Neither would come out unscathed.

---

5. God cannot be referring ultimately to physical offspring in Genesis 3:15 because Satan is an angel with no ability to reproduce. If Satan's offspring refers to spiritual children, so do Eve's. The entirety of redemptive history is the unfolding of this promise as two spiritual seeds war against each other, beginning with the murderous hostility of Cain toward Abel, both of whom were Eve's physical sons (Genesis 4). With regard to their spiritual condition, Cain was a son of the devil (1 John 3:12), while Abel was a son of God (Heb. 11:4).

6. O. Palmer Robertson writes, "To correspond to the narrowing from 'seed' to 'Satan' on the one side of the enmity, it would appear quite appropriate to expect a similar narrowing from a multiple 'seed' of woman to a singular 'he' who would champion the cause of God's enmity against Satan." *Christ of the Covenants*, 99.

But the blow inflicted to Satan would be deadly, crushing his head, while Eve's son would suffer a mere foot fracture. The imagery is of Eve's son stomping on the serpent's head and injuring his foot in the process. In their fallen condition, Adam and Eve were powerless to defeat the devil, but God was promising to do everything necessary to ensure Satan wouldn't win the day. In His grace God would raise up a Son who would deal a fatal blow to this arrogant angel.

With a word of promise, the Lord proclaimed glad tidings in the garden. "In this," writes Francis Turretin, "the wonderful mercy of God shines forth, which willed to propose on the spot the remedy of grace to Adam for healing the wound received from Satan."[7] No sooner had humankind fallen than God revealed Himself as the Deliverer, the One who both initiates and accomplishes the salvation of His helplessly fallen image bearers.

This was the inauguration of what is called the *covenant of grace*. Adam, as the representative of original humanity, had pridefully followed the serpent, breaking the covenant of works. But in astonishing grace, God promised to provide a second Adam from Eve's offspring who would be the serpent's demise, delivering prideful creatures from his clutches and reconciling them to the Creator.[8] Amazing grace! And because God desired Adam and Eve to grasp His grace, He accompanied His word of promise with a graphic sign.

Having stripped them of their fig leaves (their futile attempt at self-salvation), God Himself clothed our parents. "Also for Adam and his wife the LORD God made tunics of skin, and clothed them" (Gen. 3:21). But the only way to make "tunics of skin" is to slaughter and skin an animal. Here was nothing less than the first animal sacrifice, and God Himself was the one performing it!

---

7. Turretin, *Institutes*, 2:220.

8. Westminster Confession 7.3 states, "Man, by his fall, having made himself uncapable of life by that covenant, the Lord was pleased to make a second, commonly called the covenant of grace; wherein he freely offereth unto sinners life and salvation by Jesus Christ; requiring of them faith in him, that they may be saved."

Put yourself in Adam and Eve's proverbial shoes. You have defied the Creator. You have deified the creature. You were warned that such autonomous rebellion would result in death. And now your Creator approaches with sword drawn. You hide, preparing to be slaughtered by divine wrath. But as your Creator draws near, His sword never descends on you. Instead, it descends on an animal of His choosing. The creature's blood spills on the ground, and the butchered beast becomes the means by which God clothes you, covering over your guilt and shame. God graciously provides a substitute.

The Creator, by word and sign, placarded His grace before the first couple. Divine grace, states J. I. Packer, is "God showing goodness to persons who deserve only severity and had no reason to expect anything but severity."[9] That is precisely what God did, demonstrating immeasurable kindness toward Adam and Eve when they deserved immeasurable severity.

Grace, Grace, It's All of Grace!

During the Reformation, God's gospel kindness came to be summarized by the Latin phrase *soli gratia*. Salvation is by grace alone. There is simply no other way for corrupt creatures to be delivered from demonic captivity, delusional conceit, and divine wrath. Liberating corrupt creatures from pride and its curse requires nothing less than God and God alone!

Grace is a humbling reality. It tells us we don't deserve it and that we don't earn it. It tells us we are needy and helpless. But it is one thing to say we are saved by grace and another thing entirely to say we are saved by grace *alone*. The *alone* highlights our utter passivity in salvation. We contribute nothing; God contributes all. Our Creator did not come to Adam and Eve and tell them to try their best and He would do the rest. Instead, He promised that a representative son of Eve would come to defeat the serpent. He promised that a substitute would be slain to provide a covering for their serpentine arrogance. They were entirely powerless to deliver themselves, but

---

9. Packer, *Knowing God*, 132.

God would graciously raise up a Deliverer to restore His fallen image to humble, filial communion with Him.

If God alone initiates and accomplishes our salvation, then all that is left for us to do is to receive it. A salvation that is by grace alone (*soli gratia*) is a salvation that is received by faith alone (*sola fide*). Humility does not stop at the controlling sense of corruption. It does not wallow in the mud and mire. It does not find pleasure in doom and gloom. The lowly in spirit turn from their sin to God in desperation, crying out, "God, be merciful to me a sinner!" (Luke 18:13). The humble declare, "I cannot save myself. But praise be to God, who has graciously initiated and accomplished salvation for a prideful son of the devil like me! He has done it all, and I dare not reject His gift." The humble believe God's saving promise.

God's Grace in God's Son

Millennia would pass before this promised son of Eve would arrive on the scene of redemptive history. But in the fullness of time, He would come. Who was He? The eternal Son of God, born in human flesh (Gal. 4:4). That is, after all, what our salvation required—One who was truly God and truly man. Pride alienated the creature from the Creator, but the Son of God became the Mediator to bring the creature back into warm Father-son fellowship with the Creator. The second person of the Godhead graciously assumed our frail humanity as our covenant representative. Just as the first Adam represented the original humanity, so Jesus Christ came as the second Adam to represent the new humanity (e.g., Rom. 5:12–19; 1 Cor. 15:21–22).

The Son's mediatorial work is a precious truth to the humble, for it is the most astounding demonstration of divine grace toward corrupt creatures imaginable. And as such, it provides us with an unfathomably breathtaking, jaw-dropping, awe-inspiring picture of perfect creaturely humility.

Divine Grace through Divine Condescension

From eternity past, the Son of God dwelled in the bosom of His Father. They, together with the Spirit, ever existed in perfectly inter-penetrating, stunningly glorious, unspeakably sweet communion. The Son is God of Himself—self-existent, self-sufficient, and self-satisfied. He doesn't need you or me or any created thing. But out of the overflow of intra-Trinitarian love, He created. The Son of God is the eternal Creator and Sustainer of all (John 1:3; Col. 1:16–17). And that is what makes the apostle's words so shocking when he says of the Son that "being in the form of God, [He] did not consider it robbery to be equal with God, but made Himself of no reputa-tion, taking the form of a bondservant, and coming in the likeness of men" (Phil. 2:6–7).

Though equal with the Father and Spirit in power and glory, the Son "did not consider it robbery to be equal with God." Rather than grasping at His divine prerogatives, the Son "made Himself of no reputation," or, more literally, "emptied himself" (ESV). This was not an emptying of deity. The Son's incarnation did not result in Him becoming less than equal with God. If the incarnate Christ is less than God, He was never God to begin with.

So what does it mean for the Son to empty Himself? We are told in no uncertain terms that this voluntary self-emptying was by way not of subtraction, but of addition. He emptied Himself by "tak-ing the form of a bondservant, and coming in the likeness of men" (Phil. 2:7). The Son did not discard His deity; He took to Himself our humanity.[10] The infinite Creator became a finite creature without in any way forgoing His Creator infinity.

---

10. John Calvin helpfully explains the nature of this voluntary self-emptying: "Christ, indeed, could not divest himself of Godhead; but he kept it concealed for a time, that it might not be seen, under the weakness of the flesh. Hence he laid aside his glory in the view of men, not by lessening it, but by concealing it." *Commentaries on the Epistles of Paul the Apostle to the Philip-pians, Colossians, and Thessalonians*, trans. John Pringle (Edinburgh: Calvin Translation Society, 1851), 56–57.

This is simply beyond our ability to grasp. One of the finest articulators of the glory of the incarnation, the English theologian John Owen, admitted,

> We speak of these things in a poor, low, broken manner,—we teach them as they are revealed in the Scripture,—we labour by faith to adhere unto them as revealed; but when we come into a steady, direct view and consideration of the thing itself [the eternal Son of God becoming man], our minds fail, our hearts tremble, and we can find no rest but in a holy admiration of what we cannot comprehend. Here we are at a loss, and know that we shall be so whilst we are in this world; but all the ineffable fruits and benefits of this truth are communicated unto them that do believe.[11]

It is impossible for us to wrap our minds and hearts around this truth. But the humble embrace and believe the incarnation of the Son of God in all its mysterious wonder.

The incarnation required a descent of infinite proportions. For our purposes, it is important to ask, Was this descent of the Son a demonstration of humility? Many would say that it was the greatest demonstration of humility ever known. But that raises a more fundamental question: Can the divine be humble? Is humility an attribute of God? Certainly not, if by humility we mean the lowly spirit elicited by a controlling sense of one's creatureliness and corruption. God cannot possess the downward disposition of a Godward self-perception, for what is humility but the creature's affectionate recognition that he is not God? And God can never not be God! Thus, if a person wishes to speak of the incarnation as a demonstration of divine humility, he or she must radically redefine the term. But that is unnecessary, for there is a much more fitting word to describe the divine lowliness—condescension.

---

11. John Owen, *Meditations and Discourses on the Glory of Christ*, in *The Works of John Owen*, ed. William H. Goold (Edinburgh: Banner of Truth, 1965), 1:330.

Condescension is a term we encountered in our look at God's covenant with Adam. For the Creator to relate to His creatures always requires Him to descend to their level. Whenever and wherever God condescends, He is getting low. But He is not thereby exercising humility. Admittedly, some Bible translations refer to God humbling Himself. For example, the King James Version translates Psalm 113:5–6 this way: "Who is like unto the LORD our God, who dwelleth on high, who humbleth himself to behold the things that are in heaven, and in the earth!" But verse 6 would be better translated, "who condescends to behold the things that are in heaven, and in the earth!" This is a text teaching the ontological necessity of divine condescension if the Creator is to relate to His creation. It is not an assertion of humility in the Creator.

All throughout history God had been coming low to dwell with His people (sometimes even appearing temporarily in human form), but never had God condescended to become man, permanently wedding humanity to His deity. This, writes Owen, "is the glory of the Christian religion, and the animating soul of all evangelical truth."[12] This is the fulfillment of God's gracious promise in the garden to raise up a son of Eve who alone would defeat the serpent.

Notice that Paul does not say that the eternal Son of God "*humbled Himself*, by taking the form of a servant." Instead, he says that He "emptied himself" (Phil. 2:7 ESV). The incarnation displays the lowliness of gracious condescension, not the lowliness of creaturely humility.[13]

---

12. Owen, *Meditations and Discourses on the Glory of Christ*, 1:330. He makes this perceptive and humbling point earlier: "All [God's] respect unto the creatures, the most glorious of them, is an act of infinite condescension" (1:324).

13. Many godly men use the word *humble* to refer to the act of God incarnating Himself. My own confessional standards state, "Christ humbled himself in his conception and birth, in that, being from all eternity the Son of God, in the bosom of the Father, he was pleased in the fullness of time to become the son of man, made of a woman of low estate, and to be born of her" (Westminster Larger Catechism 47). I see no problem with this, understanding that the authors are using *humble* as a synonym for *condescend*, similar to the KJV

Divine Grace through Human Humility

Only after He emptied Himself through assuming our humanity is Christ said to possess and exercise humility. "And *being found in appearance as a man*, He humbled Himself" (Phil. 2:8). The incarnation is not the outworking of humility; humility is the outworking of the incarnation. The Son did not become man because He was humble; He became humble because He was man. Perfect humanity entails perfect humility.

Christ's humility, unlike ours, was not produced by the controlling sense of His own personal corruption, for He was not a man of unclean lips and heart as we are (2 Cor. 5:21; Heb. 4:15). He was not conceived in sin as we are (Luke 1:35). As a man, He perfectly feared God and was perfectly devoted to God (Isa. 11:1–3; Heb. 10:5–7). This fearful devotion worked itself out in a life of humble obedience. He "humbled himself by becoming obedient" (Phil. 2:8 ESV). Christ didn't say, "No right! No wrongs! No rules for me! I'm free!" Being found in human form, He possessed a controlling sense of His creatureliness. He knew Himself to be morally accountable to God. This was no cold, impersonal sense of obligation; it was the loving obligation of a Son who delighted in doing the will of His Father in comprehensive creaturely reliance (John 5:19, 30). Here, for the first time since the garden of Eden, we see the image of God rightly relating to the Original in

- perfect Godward dependence
- perfect Godward submission
- perfect Godward delight
- perfect Godward humility

Behold the incarnate Christ! And here is the marvel of the gospel: as the seed of the woman, Christ possessed this lowly spirit not as a lone individual, but as the representative of all of Eve's spiritual children. Corrupt creatures like us cannot perform a single righteous

---

translation of Psalm 113:6. But I argue that it is better to reserve the terms *humble* and *humility* for creatures.

deed by which to stand before our holy Creator. Even our best deeds are shot through with pride. But in humility Christ rendered perfect and perpetual obedience to God. He did what the first Adam failed to do, and He did so as the Mediator of fallen image bearers who put their trust in Him (Rom. 5:12–21).

But there is more. According to God's promise, Eve's Son would not obtain victory over the serpent without battle scars. Christ's humble obedience led Him to the accursed death of the cross: "And being found in human form, he humbled himself by becoming obedient to the point of death, even death on a cross" (Phil. 2:8 ESV). Roman crucifixion was the most brutal and shameful of deaths. This was the very pit of hell itself. But there was no other way to crush the serpent's head and deliver Eve's children from their prideful bondage.

The penalty of Adam's sin and our own is eternal death. Recall the words of Thomas Boston: "Are you able to satisfy the justice of God? Can you pay your own debt? Surely not: for, as He is the infinite God, whom you have offended, the punishment, being suited to the quality of the offence, must be infinite. But your punishment, or sufferings for sin, cannot be infinite in value, for you are a finite creature: therefore, they must be infinite in duration or continuance; that is, they must be eternal."[14]

As corrupt creatures, we have incurred an infinite debt. But as finite creatures, we have no ability to satisfy our Creator's infinite justice. Only God, who is infinite in glory, can pay the infinite debt of our sin. And that is precisely what the Son came to do. That is why He went to the cross. The humble Image bore the sins of proud images (2 Cor. 5:21; 1 Peter 2:24). Perfect humility died the death that our arrogance deserved. This was no mere physical death. Christ's death was a propitiation (Rom. 3:25). It was a sacrifice that satisfied God's infinite wrath against our pride. Like the beast slain to clothe our first parents, Christ came under the sword of God's justice, being forsaken by His Father and treated as if He were an arrogant son of the devil (Ps. 22:1).

---

14. Boston, *Human Nature in Its Fourfold State*, 187.

At the cross we behold a sacrifice of infinite value. Only the Creator could be of infinite value. Only the creature could be a sacrifice. And that is the wonder of the gospel—a singular person who is truly Creator and truly creature dying to reconcile the Creator to the creature. "For," explains John Stott, "the essence of sin is man substituting himself for God, while the essence of salvation is God substituting himself for man. Man asserts himself against God and puts himself where only God deserves to be; God sacrifices himself for man and puts himself where only man deserves to be. Man claims prerogatives which belong to God alone; God accepts penalties which belong to man alone."[15]

Do you see how humility is at the core of the gospel? Corrupt creatures like us assume we are the Creator, so the Creator becomes a creature, perfectly embraces that creatureliness, and dies for our arrogant denial of it. But the gospel does not end at the lowliness of crucifixion, for in God's economy, true creaturely lowliness always leads to the creature's exaltation.

The Father was so pleased with the humble sacrifice of His Son that He raised Him to the highest place and gave Him the highest name: "Therefore [because of His humility unto death] God also has highly exalted Him and given Him the name which is above every name" (Phil. 2:9). The lowly Son was lifted high in His resurrection and ascension. He, as the representative of a new humanity, obtained the heavenly life forfeited by the first Adam. The Son humbly lived, died, and rose in our skin in order to bring prideful creatures like us back into fellowship with our fatherly Creator forever.

A Christward Self-Perception

The gospel sets before us incomprehensible grace, and that grace is always and only in Christ. Salvation by grace alone (*sola gratia*) is salvation in Christ alone (*sola Christus*). There is simply no other way for arrogant images to be reunited to God in a loving bond of fellowship

---

15. John Stott, *The Cross of Christ*, 2nd ed. (Leicester, UK: Inter-Varsity, 1989), 160.

(John 14:6). There is no other name under heaven by which we can be saved from our pride and its consequences (Acts 4:12).

For corrupt creatures, the Godward self-perception of humility must always be a Christward self-perception. Postfall humility is infatuated with the God-man, Jesus Christ. It receives and rests on Him as the only Mediator between God and man. The humble know they are grossly arrogant sinners, but they equally know they are represented by a gloriously humble Savior. The lowly spirit is a believing spirit, and the object of saving faith is the incarnate, crucified, and exalted Christ.

CHAPTER 8

Foreloved Believers

The gospel is the news of the Creator's gracious condescension to bring back corrupt creatures to Himself—a condescension of infinite proportions and awesome glory. We were entirely helpless to deliver our prideful selves, so the eternal Son of God, as our Deliverer, stooped to take on humanity. Exercising impeccable creaturely humility, the God-man perfectly related to His Father, humbly fulfilling the law's precepts, and perfectly suffered for those who defied their fatherly Creator, humbly satisfying the law's penalties.

If Not Humility, Then What?

The question you may be asking is, Why? What would possibly lead the second person of the Godhead to become a man and obey, even to death, as the representative of hell-worthy children of the devil? The answer, we have seen, is not found by ascribing humility to God. The Son did not take on flesh because He was lowly in spirit, for humility is unbefitting of the Creator. Then what would cause Him to become incarnate for our sake? According to the Scriptures, the Son came down because of love. This gracious condescension was the outworking of infinite, eternal, triune love, for God is Himself love, and nowhere is His love more clearly set before us than in the incarnation and death of the Son of God (1 John 4:8–10).

Before the creation of the space-time universe, the three persons of the Godhead existed in "a state of matchless happiness," writes

John Flavel, wherein "the holy, holy, holy Father embraced the thrice holy Son with a most holy delight and love."[1] This was the happiness of "absolute, permanent, exclusive, pure, irreversible, and fully expressed devotion."[2]

God's creation of the world, and in particular His creation of man as image, was the overflow of His happy love. Man was uniquely designed to live in a Father-son communion bond with his Creator. Above and beyond this, God covenanted with His image out of a desire to establish humankind in the orbit of His loving affection forever. The great goal of the covenant of works was to confirm us in "a state of matchless happiness" in God's presence everlastingly. But Adam pridefully broke covenant. He exalted the creature above the Creator, resulting in him and all his posterity being cut off from such filial fellowship.

We ought to be shaken to the core of our beings by this Edenic conspiracy, but God was not. Our pride didn't take Him by surprise. As the author of history, our Creator knows the end from the beginning (Isa. 46:9–10). Absolutely nothing—not even the fall—happens apart from His predetermined purpose.[3] He is the one "who works all things according to the counsel of His will" (Eph. 1:11).

Before the image was ever formed from the dust, God knew that he would fall and planned a way of drawing him back into His fatherly arms. The salvation lovingly accomplished by the Son was the outworking of a loving arrangement between the persons of the Godhead before time began. It is to God's affectionate decree that we

---

1. John Flavel, *The Fountain of Life Opened Up*, in *The Works of John Flavel* (Edinburgh: Banner of Truth, 1968), 1:46–47.

2. Ferguson, *Devoted to God*, 2.

3. Westminster Confession 3.1 helpfully summarizes and clarifies the scriptural teaching: "God, from all eternity, did, by the most wise and holy counsel of his own will, freely, and unchangeably ordain whatsoever comes to pass: yet so, as thereby neither is God the author of sin, nor is violence offered to the will of the creatures; nor is the liberty or contingency of second causes taken away, but rather established."

direct our attention as we continue to pursue the downward disposition of a Godward self-perception.

God's Loving Pact

The Son's incarnate condescension and obedient humility were not plan B. These saving acts were nothing less than God's unchanging purpose. The gospel love manifest in the fullness of time is a love that transcends time as the Father, Son, and Spirit entered into an eternal agreement to save fallen image bearers. In theology, we call this the *covenant of redemption*, a timeless pact in which the Father agreed to give His Son as the Mediator, the Son agreed to carry out all that was required to mediate, and the Spirit agreed to apply the Son's mediation to the lost children of Adam.

There is certainly danger in speculatively prying into God's eternal counsel, but there is an equal danger in blatantly ignoring it. While God's eternal plan is shrouded in mystery, He has seen fit to provide glimpses of this loving arrangement throughout the Scriptures (e.g., Pss. 2:7; 110; Zech. 6:13).[4] Failing to see what God has revealed can only be to our detriment.

John 17 is one such place where the pretemporal veil is lifted. The agony of the Son's impending crucifixion drove Him to an impassioned prayer that beckons us into the inner counsel of the eternal God. Through this hallowed utterance, Jesus revealed a number of staggering truths:

- The Son existed in interpenetrating glory and loving oneness with the Father before creation (vv. 5, 21–24, 26).

- Before time the Father gave the Son a work to accomplish for the salvation of the fallen creatures given to Him (vv. 4, 6).

---

4. For a concise yet thorough treatment of this doctrine, see Guy M. Richard, "The Covenant of Redemption," in *Covenant Theology: Biblical, Theological, and Historical Perspectives*, ed. Guy Prentiss Waters, J. Nicholas Reid, and John R. Muether (Wheaton, Ill.: Crossway, 2020), 43–62.

- In time the Father sent the Son into the world to carry out this saving work (vv. 8, 25).

- The Son, through His coming and perfect obedience, accomplished salvation for His people, ensuring they would be ushered into the orbit of triune love forever (vv. 3, 20–24, 26).

Christ's work was no accident. It was not God's frazzled attempt to undo a prideful fall He didn't see coming. From eternity the Father appointed the Son as Mediator of a particular people gifted to Him. At the appointed time the Son came, declaring with the psalmist, "Behold, I have come…to do Your will, O God" (Heb. 10:7), living and dying for those who were eternally His. To what end? Christ awesomely summarizes the goal of this covenant arrangement in the final words of His prayer: "that the love with which You loved Me may be in them, and I in them" (John 17:26).

What wonder! This intra-Trinitarian agreement was not an act of cold, deterministic sovereignty. It proceeded from a warmhearted sovereignty willing to go to any length to restore intimate fellowship with rebellious creatures like us.[5] Flavel movingly draws out the affectionate communication between the Father and the Son in this pact:

Father: My Son, here is a company of poor miserable souls, that have utterly undone themselves, and now lie open to my justice! Justice demands satisfaction for them, or will satisfy itself in the eternal ruin of them: What shall be done for these souls?

Son: O my Father, such is my love to, and pity for them, that rather than they shall perish eternally, I will be responsible for them as their Surety; bring in all thy bills, that I may see what they owe thee; Lord, bring them all in, that there may be no

5. Joel Beeke notes that the center of Reformed theology (i.e., theology aligned with the Bible) is "a fatherly, sovereign God in Christ Jesus." *Living for God's Glory: An Introduction to Calvinism* (Sanford, Fla.: Reformation Trust, 2008), 41. Of the covenant of redemption, J. V. Fesko writes, "Far from a cold piece of business…the Father sends the Son in love, and the Son obeys the Father in love, and the Spirit applies the Son's work in love." *The Trinity and the Covenant of Redemption* (Fearn, Ross-shire, Scotland: Christian Focus, 2016), 193.

after-reckonings with them; at my hand shalt thou require it. I will rather choose to suffer thy wrath than they should suffer it: upon me, my Father, upon me be all their debt.

Father: But, my Son, if thou undertake for them, thou must reckon to pay the last mite, expect no abatements; if I spare them, I will not spare thee.

Son: Content, Father, let it be so; charge it all upon me, I am able to discharge it: and though it prove a kind of undoing to me, though it impoverish all my riches, empty all my treasures,...yet I am content to undertake it.[6]

If that will not impel you to adoring worship of and sweet submission to your fatherly Creator, nothing will.

What humility this eternal love of God ought to foster in us! How it should dissolve our hearts in lowly, God-fearing love.[7] The Father willed to give up His infinitely treasured Son for us. The Son willed to give up His infinite riches in heavenly glory for us. Those who grasp their creatureliness and corruption will tremble at the thought.

This astounding arrangement teaches us the vanity of all our attempts at self-salvation. No scheme can rescue us from our pride except the loving scheme of God Himself. The lowly in spirit exclaim, "What marvelous love is displayed in God's eternal plan of salvation! None but my fatherly Creator could devise a way to save my arrogant soul."

He Loves Because He Loves

The Scriptures teach that God lovingly planned to save His people before time. But what could possibly warrant this divine affection?

---

6. Flavel, *Fountain of Life*, 1:61.

7. John Owen writes, "It was from eternity that he laid in his own bosom a design for our happiness. The very thought of this is enough to make all that is within us, like the babe in the womb of Elisabeth, to leap for joy. A sense of it cannot but prostrate our souls to the lowest abasement of a humble, holy reverence, and make us rejoice before him with trembling." *Communion with God*, 2:33.

Certainly nothing in us could. Under the old covenant, God set His love on His chosen people, Israel. But why did He love them? The Lord tells Israel, "The LORD did not set His love on you nor choose you because you were more in number than any other people, for you were the least of all peoples; *but because the LORD loves you*" (Deut. 7:7–8). Do you grasp what God is saying? "I love you, Israel, because I love you." The divine love has no deeper ground than the divine love. There is nothing more ultimate that God can appeal to in order to establish or explain His affection toward His people.

God didn't set His saving love on image-bearing creatures because He was impressed by their résumés or moved by their beauty or induced by their moral uprightness. This eternal pact was "between those whose love proceeds from within themselves, without there being any lovableness in the object of this love."[8] He loved them freely (Rom. 9:13). He loved them everlastingly (Jer. 31:3). He loved them because He loved them.

Here is how the apostle Paul puts it: "For whom He foreknew, He also predestined to be conformed to the image of His Son, that He might be the firstborn among many brethren" (Rom. 8:29). The divine foreknowledge spoken of is knowledge of the most intimate sort and is best rendered *foreloved*.[9] God's eternal love is the ground of every blessing in this unbreakable chain of salvation. His preloving logically precedes His predestining. Those whom God foreloved, He chose. This is another way of saying, "*In love* he predestined us" (Eph. 1:4–5 ESV). Behind God's sovereign choice is a sovereign love that is entirely uncoerced and unelicited by its object. Love was the impetus behind the Father giving a people to the Son in eternity past.

---

8. Wilhelmus á Brakel, *The Christian's Reasonable Service*, trans. Bartel Elshout, ed. Joel R. Beeke (Grand Rapids: Reformation Heritage Books, 1993), 1:263.

9. See John Murray, *Epistle to the Romans*, 1:317. Murray argues persuasively that the foreknown are those "whom [God] set regard upon" or "whom he knew from eternity with distinguished affection and delight," concluding that such a statement "is virtually equivalent to 'whom he foreloved.'"

To be saved now is to be chosen before time, and to be chosen before time is to be eternally loved. Christians are foreloved believers.

Few realities elicit the downward disposition of a Godward self-perception like God's foreloving. The Creator does not have His arm twisted by the creature into loving. The creature is entirely passive here, for you and I cannot be active when we don't even exist! And that is the point. God is not coerced into loving by good looks or IQ or nice manners or faithful church attendance. Before any of those things were possible, He loved (Rom. 9:10–21). The humble acknowledge they can do nothing to earn God's heart. In fact, they go further. The lowly in spirit recognize that if God's loving election depended on them and their performance, they never would have earned His heart. Charles Spurgeon confessed, "I believe the doctrine of election, because I am quite sure that if God had not chosen me, I would never have chosen him; and I am sure he chose me before I was born, or else he never would have chosen me afterward."[10] None but the lowly can speak like that.

Beloved in the Beloved

As we have seen, the Godward self-perception of postfall humility is ever and always a Christward self-perception. It should be no surprise, then, that God's eternal foreloving is *in Christ*. Paul stresses this in his opening doxology in Ephesians:

- God "chose us *in Him* before the foundation of the world" (1:4).
- God "predestined us to adoption as sons *by Jesus Christ*" (v. 5).
- God "made us accepted *in the Beloved*" (v. 6).

God's elect are eternally beloved in the Beloved. The Father loves believers with the affection He has for His only begotten Son.

---

10. Charles H. Spurgeon, *C. H. Spurgeon Autobiography*, vol. 1, *The Early Years, 1834–1859* (Edinburgh: Banner of Truth, 1962), 166.

The humble do not dare to explore God's eternal counsel without Christward spectacles. The intense, inscrutable affection of the Father toward His only begotten Son reached corrupt creatures because from eternity past they were considered "in Him" (Eph. 1:4). Or, to use the word of Christ, they were eternally "given" to Him (John 10:29; 17:6). Calvin pastorally advises us that "we shall not find assurance of our election in ourselves; and not even God the Father, if we conceive of him as severed from his Son. Christ, then, is the mirror wherein we must, and without self-deception may, contemplate our own election."[11] It is only through exercising humble faith in the Mediator Jesus Christ that we can come to see ourselves as eternally loved.

Are you looking to Christ? Have you come to see yourself as a fallen, delusional, and hopelessly corrupt creature who is damned apart from the incarnate, crucified, and risen Son of God? If you have, you are a foreloved believer. And God, as your fatherly Creator and Redeemer, wants you to bask in His sovereign affection toward you. As Geerhardus Vos so beautifully explains, God's love toward us "means that in the most literal sense He concentrates all the light and warmth of His affection, all the prodigious wealth of its resources, his endless capacity of delight, upon the heart-to-heart union between the pious and Himself. And what God for His part brings into this union has a generosity, a sublime abandon, an absoluteness, that, measured by human analogies, we can only designate as the highest and purest type of devotion."[12]

No wonder the apostle claimed that God's gospel love "passes knowledge" (Eph. 3:19). Oh for greater strength of soul to comprehend it!

11. Calvin, *Institutes*, 3.24.5.
12. Geerhardus Vos, "Jeremiah's Plaint and Its Answer," in *Redemptive History and Biblical Interpretation: The Shorter Writings of Geerhardus Vos*, ed. Richard B. Gaffin Jr. (Phillipsburg, N.J.: P&R, 1980), 296.

I Am Eternally Loved

We sat across the table from one another, plates of eggs and bacon largely untouched. My seminary professor patiently listened as I poured out my heart, expressing the anxieties that plagued my day-to-day existence. Finally, after some time, he gently offered his diagnosis: "Nick, I think you have a father wound."

His words caught me completely by surprise. It was true—my parents had divorced when I was a toddler. Since then, my biological father had not been an active presence in my life. I hadn't seen or talked to him. I didn't know him, and he didn't know me. But I had convinced myself that this missing relationship had not affected me. After all, my mom had remarried when I was in elementary school, and the man she married legally adopted me and loved me. Besides that, how could someone I hadn't interacted with since I was a one-year-old impact me in any significant way? I was skeptical, to say the least. But over the upcoming weeks, I began to recognize that I had a deep, festering father wound. The absence of my biological dad had left the unarticulated question reverberating in my soul: "Why doesn't he love me?"[13]

I was wounded—hungry for the blessing of my dad and insecure without it. Life was an anxious quest for affirmation, acceptance, and affection, all of which I pursued by way of performance. I was a professional people pleaser, working for the applause of others. Such was my prideful, creature-exalting attempt to deal with my wounded heart. But it was all in vain. Nothing in the created order could heal this laceration of soul.

There is one transcendent truth, however, that has liberated me since that breakfast conversation—the eternal love of God. In the gospel, my fatherly Creator proclaims, "Before you ever existed, I

---

13. John Sowers explains, "When a dad's not there, what he's actually saying to you, that you hear loud and clear even if he never says it, is, 'You're not worth it to me to be here.'" As quoted in John Finch with Blake Atwood, *The Father Effect: Hope and Healing from a Dad's Absence* (New York: Hachette, 2017), 44.

loved you. Before you ever performed, I loved you. Before you ever achieved, I loved you."

God's eternal counsel is not some esoteric obscurity. It is not a truth reserved for PhD theologians. God's declaration "I have loved you with an everlasting love" (Jer. 31:3) is Christianity 101. "In the unlimitable round of [God's] timeless existence," writes Vos, "[you] have never been absent from nor uncared for by Him."[14] If you are a believer, you are eternally loved by God.

At first I struggled to affirm this with particular reference to myself. But by the Spirit's gracious work and word, my lips came to profess the awesome utterance, "God loves *me* with an affection that never began and will never end." The personal pronoun is vital. He loves *me*. This is what it is to have a Christward self-perception. The humble not only affirm God's love for sinners in general, but they see themselves before God's hidden counsel. Having exercised faith in the Son of God and having received salvation, they come to grasp that such faith and salvation are the result of a foreloving God who possesses an affection toward them that transcends time. Can you say that about yourself?

Sadly, there are Christians who question the appropriateness of such a self-perception. "Isn't it presumptuous to assert that God loves *me*?" they retort. Such a question gives the appearance of humility, but could it actually be pride clothed in pious garb? The aversion to personal pronouns (e.g., I, me, my) would have been foreign to the apostle who confidently declared, "I live by faith in the Son of God, who loved *me* and gave Himself for *me*" (Gal. 2:20). Is it presumption for my son Owen to assert, "*My* dad loves *me*"? Not in the least. He is *my* boy! I express my love to him daily because I want him to know he has my heart. In fact, I would be hurt and dishonored if Owen went about his days questioning my affection and telling others, "I know Dad is loving, but I'm just not sure he loves me."

---

14. Vos, "Jeremiah's Plaint and Its Answer," 298.

The statement "God loves me" could certainly be presumptuous, but not if you are receiving and resting on Christ alone for salvation. God wants His children to know His love. He is severely dishonored when believers doubt it under the guise of an alleged humility. On the contrary, His ears are delighted to hear corrupt creatures personally praise, "For great is your steadfast love toward *me*; you have delivered *my* soul from the depths of Sheol" (Ps. 86:13 ESV).

Pride Distorts the Loving Creator

Why is it that we so often doubt the love of God? The root of all our doubts is pride. Think for a moment about the serpent's tactic in the garden. He deceived our first parents into misperceiving their fatherly Creator as stingy, uncaring, distant, and cold. We could compress his lies into four simple words—*God doesn't love you!* Adam and Eve misperceived God as unloving, and they misperceived themselves as unloved. Pride projects God as an abusive, miserly Father.

If the love of God is foreign to you, please keep wrestling with the truths of this chapter and the last. In the gospel God projects His true character as the fatherly Creator who so desires to bring His sinful image back into His embrace that He sends the Son of His love down to live as a finite creature and die as if He were a fallen creature. No matter who you are or what you have done, God lovingly offers Himself to you in the gospel. And only one thing could keep you from receiving that love.

Pride.

In our arrogance, we refuse to come to terms with this deep love of God. We say things like this:

- "God could never love someone like me."
- "God could never love someone with a past like mine."
- "God cannot be love given the unbearable trauma I have faced."
- "God cannot be love given the great evil in the world."

Please understand I am in no way downplaying the devastating wickedness in the world and in our hearts. The Bible doesn't whitewash these realities. But neither does it see them as contradictory to God's fatherly affection. God comes in the gospel, offering Himself to us in love. And all of our excuses for not embracing Him come back to this—we are arrogant. We have listened to the serpent. We have exalted ourselves above our Creator, dictating who and how He can love and assuming He can't love us given our past or present condition. We need the downward disposition of a Christward self-perception if we would relish in God's unfathomable heart.

Love Is the Ground and the Goal

God knew our pride would result in us being cast out from the sphere of His intra-Trinitarian affection. But before the creation and fall, the Father gifted a people to His Son, and the Son embraced them as His own. In love, our Creator schemed to do everything necessary to restore His soon-to-fall images to the enjoyment of His tripersonal delight. Love was the ground and the goal, for love possesses a holy dissatisfaction until it is received and enjoyed by its object.

The humble perceive themselves as eternally foreloved in Christ. Possessing a controlling sense of their creatureliness, they worshipfully bow before God's sovereign decree. They marvel that God, as the architect of history, would draw up a plan to live in unending communion with children of dust like them. Possessing a controlling sense of their corruption, they are entirely stunned that God would set His delight on their prideful persons. They are persuaded that nothing in them elicited the divine affection.

Beloved in the Beloved—that is humility's boast.

CHAPTER 9

Adopted Believers

Before entering gospel ministry, I had the privilege of working for an adoption agency. As I mentioned in the last chapter, my stepfather adopted me, so I have always had a heart for adoption. But I had no idea how time consuming, emotionally taxing, and financially draining the adoption process was.

It all begins with an adoption plan as the couple, with the help of the agency, puts into writing the who, when, where, and how of their future adoption. That detailed plan gives way to a nearly endless flood of interviews, paperwork, and training sessions. Oh, and don't forget, along with all of that, the couple will fork out tens of thousands of dollars to cover all the expenses. Why would anyone subject themselves to such a costly ordeal? The answer, in the best cases, is quite simple. A couple's hearts are set on a child. They love that little girl and are willing to do whatever it takes to get her home. They see the planning and paying as the necessary precursors to the adoption being finally realized.

As we saw in the previous chapter, our loving Creator eternally planned to rescue His fallen creatures. The goal of this rescue operation was adoption. "In love he predestined us for adoption to himself as sons through Jesus Christ" (Eph. 1:4–5 ESV). Before the foundation of the world, God affectionately determined the who, when, where, and how of His adoptive purpose. But this eternal arrangement was not in itself sufficient, any more than a couple's adoption plan is all that is needed to bring the adoption to pass. Once the plan was made, it had to be executed. And so it was that "when the fullness of the time had come, God sent forth His Son, born of a woman, born under the law, to redeem those who were under the law, that we might receive the adoption as sons" (Gal. 4:4–5). The Son of God condescended, becoming the offspring of the woman, who, in humble obedience, crushed the serpent's head. Here is a costliness we cannot begin to fathom! According to plan, the infinitely valuable Son came to pay all that was necessary to transfer us from Satan's household to God's.

Christ's incarnation, death, and resurrection, however, were not the conclusion of the adoption process. Though arranged in Christ and accomplished by Him, this saving purpose still needs application. All the paperwork is signed and notarized. All payments have been received. The house is furnished and ready. But the children still need to be brought into their newfound home. That is precisely what God does when He saves us through the gospel. According to His eternal arrangement and on the basis of Christ's redemptive accomplishment, He ushers us into His house and embraces us in His fatherly arms. For fallen sinners like us, this is the beginning of humility. Before the Spirit's application of salvation, we are enslaved to serpentine pride. But in God's lovingkindness, when we are brought from Satan's prison into God's palace, we begin to grow in the downward disposition of a Godward self-perception.

A Truth Worth Shouting About

My oldest son, who was a baby at the time, was sleeping in the room above me. It was a peaceful summer day, and I was making the most of it by reading John Murray's classic *Redemption Accomplished and Applied*. I had never read anything like it before. It was riveting! On this particular afternoon, I slowly perused the chapter entitled "Union with Christ."[1] Murray had told me of regeneration,

---

1. John Murray, *Redemption Accomplished and Applied* (Grand Rapids: Eerdmans, 1955), 161–73.

justification, adoption, sanctification, and perseverance, and now, in this crowning chapter, he was demonstrating how all of these saving blessings come from a singular source—Spirit-wrought attachment to Christ. My reading in that hour was worship. I was seeing and savoring my Lord, clothed in all of His benefits. At one point, my affections were so stirred by this vision that I stood up and shouted for joy at the top of my lungs. This was not a carefully articulated declaration of praise. It was a happy roar erupting from a heart that was amazed. Unfortunately, it was a shout that awoke my napping boy, resulting in a less-than-happy cry and bringing the hallowed moment quickly to an end.

The most fundamental truth about believers could be summed up in two words—*in Christ*. If you don't believe me, set aside a few hours to work through Paul's letters, jotting down every instance where the phrase is found. It is everywhere. Every spiritual blessing for believers comes to them through union with the exalted Christ (Eph. 1:3).

- We are regenerated in Christ (Eph. 2:5).
- We are justified in Christ (Rom. 8:1; Phil. 3:9).
- We are adopted in Christ (Rom. 8:15; Gal. 4:6).
- We are sanctified in Christ (1 Cor. 1:2; Col. 3:1–3).
- We are preserved in Christ (Rom. 8:37–39).

Apart from vital union with Christ by the Spirit, we are lost. This is why Calvin begins his treatment of the application of redemption by telling us, "First, we must understand that as long as Christ remains outside of us, and we are separated from him, all that he has suffered and done for the salvation of the human race remains useless and of no value to us."[2] But when Christ dwells within us and we in Him, we become the recipients of every blessing He came to procure, for Christ "became for us wisdom from God—and righteousness and sanctification and redemption" (1 Cor. 1:30). Such a reality warrants a shout! But it also warrants a lowly spirit, for Paul

---

2. Calvin, *Institutes*, 3.1.1.

tells us that the Father has made Christ to be everything in our salvation "that, as it is written, 'He who glories, let him glory in the LORD'" (1 Cor. 1:31). Those who possess this Christward self-perception are stripped of vainglory. The humble glory in Christ alone.

Arturo Toscanini, the famous Italian conductor, once led his orchestra in a flawless performance of Beethoven's Ninth Symphony. It was breathtaking. And at the close, the crowd applauded profusely. After a lengthy standing ovation and the conductor's numerous bows, he turned to address his orchestra: "Gentlemen! Gentlemen! Gentlemen!" Securing their attention, he continued, "Gentlemen, I am nothing; you are nothing; Beethoven is everything, everything, everything!"[3]

That is humility. Gospel humility cries with adoring intensity, "Ladies and gentlemen, I am nothing; you are nothing; Jesus is everything, everything, everything!"

Christ is everything in the arrangement of salvation. Christ is everything in the accomplishment of salvation. Christ is everything in the application of salvation. Truly, Christ is all in all!

Behold What Manner of Love

We can sometimes perceive union with Christ as an impersonal bond or an aloof legal transaction. But that could not be further from the truth. Our persons are wed to Christ's person by the Spirit's person. This union is profoundly personal, and it results in a depth of fellowship beyond anything this world can offer. Murray writes, "There is no communion among men that is comparable to fellowship with Christ—he communes with his people and his people commune with him in conscious reciprocal love."[4]

The affectionate communion that Christ came to restore between God and His fallen image comes to realization through this

---

3. R. Kent Hughes references this story with similar application in *Genesis: Beginning and Blessing*, Preaching the Word Commentary (Wheaton, Ill.: Crossway, 2004), 607.

4. John Murray, *Redemption Accomplished and Applied*, 169.

saving bond. "In a day of converting grace, in Christ's marriage-day," writes Thomas Boston, "there is a glorious transmigration of souls betwixt Christ and believers."[5] All that Christ is becomes ours, and all that we are becomes Christ's in a bond of "conscious reciprocal love." Believers, through the Mediator, become the recipients and reciprocators of God's steadfast love. If you have been waiting for permission, now is an appropriate time to stand up and shout!

This restored fellowship is a family fellowship, for through our union with Christ, God formally adopts us. The Spirit by whom we are bound to Christ is "the Spirit of adoption" (Rom. 8:15; see also Gal. 4:6). Through His indwelling presence, we become the children of God. Through faith we are ushered into God's house and lavished with His love: "Behold what manner of love the Father has bestowed on us, that we should be called children of God!" (1 John 3:1).

God doesn't finalize the adoption and bring us into His home only to then say, "As you well know, I am quite busy keeping the universe running. So please stay in your room, mind your own business, and don't bother Me unless it is an emergency." We have the tendency to perceive God in this way—distant and disinterested. But it is a misperception. He is our loving Creator and Redeemer. He is our affectionate heavenly Father. His heart is tender toward us. He desires intimate fellowship with us. That is why He created us in His image. That is why He saves us in His Son.

Often in our thinking, adoption takes a backseat to the blessings of justification, regeneration, and sanctification. But out of all the riches that are ours in Christ, none deserves our attention more than adoption. J. I. Packer classifies adoption as "the highest privilege that the gospel offers: higher even than justification."[6] That is because our justification reconciles us to God as righteous Judge, but our adoption reunites us to God as large-hearted Father.

---

5. Thomas Boston, "Christ the Life of the Believer," in *The Complete Works of Thomas Boston* (Stoke-on-Trent, UK: Tentmaker Publications, 2002), 4:239.

6. Packer, *Knowing God*, 206.

We are prodigals by nature. We have abandoned our fatherly Creator's house and squandered His blessings. We have proudly played the fool in Adam. But when we finally come to our senses, we find our Creator ready to embrace us, kiss us, and bless us (see Luke 15:11–32). How could this be? Only through our elder Brother, Jesus Christ—we become adopted sons and daughters through the eternal Son of God. The very love with which the Father loves Christ is the love that He showers on all who enter into Christ by faith. And the humble bask in it. The love of God is their joy and crown. It is their life and strength.

If you possess a Christward self-perception, you know yourself as an eternally loved child of God in Christ. This is the core identity of all who eye the God-man by faith. How such a self-perception ought to melt us in lowliness! What undeserved love! What unspeakable kindness! Surely no one who grasps God's adoptive grace would dare think, "I must be something pretty great for God to love me like this!" No, God's unfathomable heart impels us to tell anyone who will listen, "Behold what kind of love the Father has lavished on me, that I, a hell-worthy son of the devil, would become a heaven-worthy son of God!"

Children Rightly Related to God

But that raises an important question. How can God welcome hopelessly guilty, hell-worthy sinners into His holy family? Would that not compromise His moral purity? It would, unless there was a way for Him to justly remove our guilt and consume our hell. As we have seen, that is precisely what the righteous Son of God condescended to do. Christ came as the representative of those given to Him by the Father, bearing their guilt and suffering their hell on the cross. As an infinitely valuable sacrifice, He drank dry the cup of God's wrath in their place.

When the Spirit of adoption unites us to the Son, we become partakers of everything Christ purchased in His life and His death. That means the moment of our adoption is the moment of our justification. Bringing us into His house, our fatherly Redeemer gives us a new record (Rom. 8:1).

When we receive and rest on Christ and His finished work, God no longer counts our sins against us. He declares us *forgiven*. Our moral record is no longer racked with a debt we cannot pay because Christ paid it all:

Blessed is he whose transgression is forgiven,
Whose sin is covered.
Blessed is the man to whom the LORD does not impute iniquity,
And in whose spirit there is no deceit. (Ps. 32:1–2)

But God's children do not just have their record wiped clean in Christ. God doesn't merely declare His children *not guilty*; He positively declares them *righteous*. Believers are found in Christ "not having [their] own righteousness, which is from the law, but that which is through faith in Christ" (Phil. 3:9). By faith not only are our sins removed from us but Christ's righteousness is imputed to us. Spirit-worked faith receives Christ, writes Theodore Beza, "in such a way that it unites and knits us together with Him to be partakers of all the goodness which He has—He, who being granted and imputed to us, is fully sufficient to make us perfect and accepted as righteous before God."[7]

The righteousness of justification is outside of us. It is Christ's righteousness. We don't perform the righteousness that justifies us any more than Christ performed the sin that crucified Him. God legally imputes, or credits, Christ's righteousness to our records (see Paul's extended treatment of this in Rom. 3:21–5:21). He declares the guilty to be guiltless because they are in Christ. He declares the unrighteous to be righteous because they are in Christ. "For He made Him who knew no sin to be sin for us, that we might become the righteousness of God *in Him*" (2 Cor. 5:21).

7. See James T. Dennison Jr., *Reformed Confessions of the 16th and 17th Centuries in English Translation*, vol. 2, *1552–1566* (Grand Rapids: Reformation Heritage Books, 2010), 254.

Justification elicits humility because we are accounted righteous on the basis of nothing we have done. We have no ability to deliver ourselves from the law's penalties. We have no ability to render perfect obedience to the law's precepts. The righteous record requisite to live in God's family is not the result of our person and performance. Christ is our righteousness. Therefore, all the glory goes to Him!

The reception of this affectionate gift of righteousness constrains the heart to love Christ. Those who have a controlling sense of their corruption treasure the righteous Son. Do you remember the sinful woman who anointed our Lord before His death? She sensed her depth of depravity and saw in Christ a depth of righteous mercy answerable to her plight. In a most remarkable moment, she approached Jesus with a jar of precious ointment in her hands "and stood at His feet behind Him weeping; and she began to wash His feet with her tears, and wiped them with the hair of her head; and she kissed His feet and anointed them with the fragrant oil" (Luke 7:38). How stunningly beautiful is Christ-exalting humility! This woman loved Jesus much because Jesus had forgiven her much (v. 47). Her sense of personal sin and divine grace drove her to lowly devotion to Christ. The apostle Paul, who had once been a proud Pharisee, understood this well. Christ's righteousness had led him to "count all things loss for the excellence of the knowledge of Christ Jesus [his] Lord" (Phil. 3:8).

God's children do not boast in their own religious pedigree. They have been stripped of human merit and human-centered hope. They understand that their right to all the privileges of the children of God is due to the saving righteousness of their elder Brother alone. They glory in Him.

Children Rightly Reflecting God

A young couple adopting a child from the foster care system is typically in for a difficult journey. All his life this boy has bounced from family to family, never knowing the stability of a devoted father and mother. But now he is brought into a permanent home where he is loved as family. His newfound parents don't love him and accept him because he has his act together. They love him because they love him. Given such unconditional love, it might be tempting to think it will be happily ever after once the adoption is finalized. But that is not the case. This boy carries years of baggage from his former life. It will take time for him to learn to trust his new mom and dad and for his beliefs and behavior to change. He will run away from the home on a number of occasions. He will say and do hateful things that make his mom cry. While he becomes a part of the family the moment the papers are signed, it will take a long time for him to reflect the family. But after months and years of living in a loving bond with his adoptive parents, this boy slowly begins to look, think, talk, and act like them.

When through union with Christ God welcomes us into our new home and gives us a new record, He simultaneously transforms us to reflect Him. That is, after all, what it is to be image of God and why He has recreated us in that image in our salvation (Eph. 4:24; Col. 3:10). The Bible calls this *sanctification*—the work of God by which He sets us apart from the world so that we might be entirely devoted to Him. Similar to earthly adoption, this transformation has both initial and ongoing dimensions. Our sanctification as the children of God is both *definitive* and *progressive*.[8]

Our separation from the world occurs in its once-for-all, definitive sense the moment we are united to Christ. This is why the Bible refers to Christians as "saints" (i.e., "holy ones" or "set apart ones") and "those who are sanctified in Christ Jesus" (1 Cor. 1:2). Through our union with Christ, we are delivered from the enslaving mastery of sin. For "our old man was crucified with Him, that the body of sin might be done away with, that we should no longer be slaves of sin" (Rom. 6:6). We who once could not submit to God because we were held fast in the grip of pride are now freed to humbly bow before our fatherly Creator. We are taken out of the fleshly world order and

---

8. The term "definitive sanctification" is taken from John Murray, "Definitive Sanctification," in *Collected Writings of John Murray* (Edinburgh: Banner of Truth, 1977), 2:277–84.

brought into the family of God, having the rules of God's house written on our hearts (Jer. 31:33). And this is entirely a work of grace. We could not deliver ourselves from sin's corrupting power any more than the adopted boy could deliver himself from the foster care system. God sets us apart in Christ. He writes His law on our hearts in Christ. He causes us to die to sin in Christ. Thus, all the glory goes to God in Christ for this definitive work of transformation.

Believers have died to sin once for all (Rom. 6:11), but there is still need to "not let sin reign in your mortal body, that you should obey it in its lusts" (v. 12). Sanctification has an ongoing—even lifelong—dimension. We may no longer be in sin's slave house, but sin is still in us. We carry into our new life the arrogant baggage of our former life. We often doubt whether our new Father can be trusted. And sometimes we even think about leaving the home and going back to our former family in Adam. But through our loving spiritual bond with God, we are progressively changed. We begin to conform to the family rules. We begin to delight in our Father and elder Brother. God is working in us (Phil. 2:13) to fulfill His foreloving purpose: "For whom He foreknew, He also predestined to be conformed to the image of His Son, that He might be the firstborn among many brethren" (Rom. 8:29). According to plan, we grow downward to reflect the humble Son of God.

The lowly Christ is not only the power behind our transformation but also the pattern. John Colquhoun beautifully summarizes it this way: "Christ is the principle of his life from whom, the pattern of his life according to whom, and the end of it to whom, he lives."[9] Through His loving care, instruction, and discipline, the Father progressively strips us of our God-denying pride so that we will be entirely devoted to Him (1 Thess. 5:23–24). The image of God is being progressively restored in believers as the sons and daughters of God. To be a member of God's household is to be sanctified in Christ, freed from the

---

9. John Colquhoun, *A Treatise on the Law and the Gospel* (Grand Rapids: Reformation Heritage Books, 2009), 233.

bondage of pride, that we will grow more and more in the lowly spirit of our elder Brother, Jesus Christ.

The Core of a Christward Self-Perception

If humility is the greatest virtue, and if this downward disposition is produced by a Godward self-perception, and if a postfall Godward self-perception must be a Christward self-perception, then one of the most vital questions we can ever ask is, What is the essence of a Christward self-perception? Here is the answer this book has been building up to: *I am an eternally loved child of God, justified and sanctified in Christ Jesus, to the praise of my Father's glory.*

For quite some time, I have made this sentence one of the first things I tell myself when I wake up in the morning. When I catch myself seeking to root my identity in anything else during the day, I tell myself again. I just can't preach this statement to my soul too frequently.

If you are a believer in the Lord Jesus, this is how you ought to perceive yourself: an eternally loved child of God, justified and sanctified in Christ Jesus, to the praise of your Father's glory.

Write it on your bathroom mirror. Tape it on the dashboard of your car. Tell it to yourself throughout each day. Seek to get this reality emblazoned on your soul. Nothing will produce the downward disposition of humility like this singular sentence being increasingly applied to your heart by the Holy Spirit. Nothing will promote humble, reverent love for God like understanding His affection for you revealed in the manifold blessings that are yours in the crucified and risen Son of God. As the Dutch theologian Herman Witsius once proclaimed, "That stupendous love of God, by which he gives himself to the soul for its salvation, when it is apprehended by faith, and represented to the believer in its true light, kindles surprising flames of reciprocal love."[10]

---

10. Herman Witsius, *Sacred Dissertations on the Apostles' Creed*, trans. Donald Fraser (1823; repr., Grand Rapids: Reformation Heritage Books, 2010), 1:117.

Here is what humility is all about—the restoration and perfection of loving fellowship with our fatherly Creator. And it can only be had by a Christward self-perception. "Eternally loved child of God" is writ large over this downward disposition. God's undying affection beckons us low as our souls are raised to affectionately exult in the Father, Son, and Holy Spirit.

PART 4

Ecclesiastical Humility

ecclesiastical: pertaining to the church
We are devoted, imperfect, and missional members.

CHAPTER 10

Devoted Members

Our individualistic culture shapes us more than we care to admit. The modern maxim calls us to find ourselves not through embracing community, but through escaping community. Never in the history of humanity has this been the case. Our age claims "that we can develop ourselves," writes Tim Keller, "only by looking inward, by detaching and leaving home, religious communities, and all other requirements so that we can make our own choices and determine who we are for ourselves."[1] Few ideas pose a greater threat to humility than this, and yet we must confess that this radical vision of self-actualization divorced from God and others has made massive inroads into popular Christian thought.

When the actor Chris Pratt was called on the carpet for being a member of a church allegedly espousing a biblical view of gender and sexuality, he responded, "My faith is important to me, but no church defines me or my life, and I'm not a spokesman for any church or any group of people. My values define who I am."[2] How many Christians read Pratt's words without giving them a second thought? We have been subconsciously wired to think that being defined by a community of people is a form of bondage. We have been duped into

---

1. Timothy Keller, *Making Sense of God: Finding God in the Modern World* (New York: Penguin, 2018), 119.
2. Quoted in Mohler, *Gathering Storm*, 26.

perceiving ourselves as mere individuals who represent no one but ourselves and are represented by no one but ourselves. It is possible in our consideration of humility to give sway to this individualistic mentality. We may not succumb to our culture's outright rejection of God, but a Godward self-perception could easily be conceived as a "me-and-God" kind of religion. But biblical humility knows nothing of this. To know yourself in relation to God is to know yourself in relation to others. Whether under the covenant of works in Adam or the covenant of grace in Christ, no man is an island. When according to His eternal affection God adopts us in Christ, we are brought into a family. We become "members of the household of God" (Eph. 2:19). God's family defines us. God's family is represented by us. The downward disposition of a Christward self-perception cannot fail to reckon with this.

And They Devoted Themselves…

When Jesus ascended into heaven, He left behind a band of around 120 followers (Acts 1:15). Contrary to expectation, however, the departure of their Master did not lead these disciples to depart from one another. They held fast to each other as members of a singular community with a united vision and pursuit. And when through the Spirit's mighty ministry thousands were brought to faith on the day of Pentecost, these new believers were not baptized and then bid farewell. They were "added" to the church (2:41). For Luke, being added to the church is identical to being "added to the Lord" (5:14; 11:24). There is simply no category in the New Testament for someone vitally attached to Christ who is not also attached to His body. To be an adopted child of God and not to live in God's house or brush shoulders with God's children is a contradiction of the highest order. A humble faith in Christ will bear the fruit of a living and loving connection to Christ's church.

That is what happened in Jerusalem on the day of Pentecost. Christ "added to the church daily those who were being saved" (Acts 2:47). These new believers were not merely added to the church's rolls; they became actively engaged in the life of the body. "And they devoted themselves to the apostles' teaching and the fellowship, to the breaking of bread and the prayers" (v. 42 ESV). God had humbled them through the gospel, and it resulted in them becoming devoted members of His house.

Devoted is a striking word. The verb literally means "to continue to do something with intense effort."[3] These represented, foreloved, and adopted believers were pouring themselves into the life of the local church. Their Christward gaze had not produced a "me-and-God" religion; it had produced an "us-and-God" religion.

Lowly Consecration

The extent to which our individualistic age has shaped us can be measured in part by how we read our Bibles. For example, when most Western Christians read Romans 12:1—"I beseech you therefore, brethren, by the mercies of God, that you present your bodies a living sacrifice, holy, acceptable to God, which is your reasonable service"—they read it as a paradigm for an individual's personal sanctification—"Paul is exhorting me as an individual Christian to consecrate myself to God." There is some truth to this. The corporate dimension of the Christian life does not swallow up the uniqueness and the responsibility of the individual. But Paul did not write this letter to an individual; he wrote to the church at Rome (Rom. 1:7). And here he makes an appeal to a plurality of "brethren" to offer up a plurality of "bodies" as a singular "sacrifice." This exhortation is not primarily about me and my personal spirituality; it is more fundamentally about us and our corporate spirituality. The church is a body of distinct individuals who have given themselves over to their fatherly Creator in loving fear.

The "therefore" is of great significance in Romans 12:1. The apostle has spent the last eleven chapters of his letter setting forth the precise truths we have examined in previous chapters. He has provided a most comprehensive and devastating account of the creature's prideful rebellion and helpless condition under God's

---

3. Louw and Nida, *Greek-English Lexicon of the New Testament*, 68.68.

wrath (1:18–3:20). He has expounded on the believer's justification, adoption, sanctification, and glorification through his or
her representative, Jesus Christ, rooting it all in God's eternal love
(3:21–8:39). He has grappled with God's all-wise plan to cause His
salvation to reach the ends of the earth (9:1–11:32). And all of this
has constrained him to God-fearing worship: "Oh, the depth of the
riches both of the wisdom and knowledge of God!" (11:33). With
the glory of God in Christ looming large, he proceeds to make his
appeal: "Beloved church, you were once bound fast in pride on a
wide road leading to eternal destruction. But God delivered you in
Jesus Christ and brought you into His loving family. This was no
accident; it was according to His eternal plan to the praise of His
glory. *Therefore*, give yourselves unreservedly to Him!"

The downward disposition of a Christward self-perception
beckons us to Godward consecration. You simply cannot possess
a controlling sense of creatureliness, corruption, and redemption
without being led to the altar. While pride sacrifices God on the altar
of self, humility sacrifices self on the altar of God.

Self-sacrifice is *the* fundamental act of new covenant worship,
what the New King James Version translates as "reasonable service"
(Rom. 12:1). Old covenant worshipers didn't dare approach God
apart from a slain sacrifice, and we dare not approach God by word,
prayer, praise, and sacrament apart from giving ourselves unreservedly to Him, for we do not worship in Spirit and truth if our lives are
not humbly offered up to our God.

Can such be said of you? Is there any part of your life you are
unwilling to give to God? Pride, with its distorted view of God, is the
ground of our hesitancy to surrender all to Him.

The humble church is a body of believing sinners who "live
no longer for themselves, but for Him who died for them and rose
again" (2 Cor. 5:15). This is the foundation of their life together. It
is the foundation of everything they do. If this is lacking, all is for
nothing. A church may be bustling with activity, but where such
Godward consecration is absent, God's blessing will be absent. He
delights in and honors the humble, who recognize they are not their

own and live accordingly (1 Cor. 6:19–20). The church of His good pleasure consists of those who with one voice declare, "Lord, as the recipients of Your free grace, here we are. Our minds are Yours. Our hearts are Yours. Our lips are Yours. Our hands and feet are Yours. Take us and use us. Glorify Yourself in and through us." Humility before God wed to a loving fear of God results in a people entirely given to God.

Lowly Transformation

Consecration to God entails bowing before His word, for "submission to the unconditional sovereignty of God is seen practically in submission to the authority and sufficiency of His holy Word!"[4] That is why the early church gave itself indefatigably to "the apostles' doctrine" (Acts 2:42). The words of the apostles, as the inspired bearers of Christ's revelation, were nothing less than the words of the God-man. The humble church submits to Christ's boundless reign by submitting to Christ's boundless word.

Our age stamps *arrogant* across the forehead of anyone who would claim to be in possession of absolute truth. But in actuality, "believing God at His Word is the most humble thing Christians can do."[5] The denial of Christ's word or the relativizing of it is the height of creaturely pride. "Did God really say?"—that is pride's pet query. But the humble in Christ devote themselves to unwavering adherence to the Scriptures.

It is by this word, especially in its preached form, that the church is not only initially formed but continually transformed (1 Peter 1:22–2:3).[6] The apostle commands us to "be transformed by the renewing of your mind" (Rom. 12:2). Again, note that the command ("be transformed") and the personal pronoun ("your") are

---

4. Ian Hamilton, *What Is Experiential Calvinism?* (Grand Rapids: Reformation Heritage Books, 2015), 29.

5. Hutchinson, *Rediscovering Humility*, 49.

6. For the relationship between the preached word and God's assembled people, see Christopher Ash, *The Priority of Preaching* (Fearn, Ross-shire, Scotland: Christian Focus, 2009), 75–106.

plural. This is not a command calling on isolated individuals to seek mind-renewing transformation in the privacy of their homes. This is a command to the church, and interestingly, it is a passive command. We are being commanded to do something that we ourselves do not and cannot do.

This can be illustrated by a common, well-intentioned practice. When we hear that someone is in the hospital, we often send a "Get Well Soon" card. Think about it: How helpful or encouraging is it when we tell someone who is bedridden in the hospital to "get well soon," as if she has some ability to eradicate disease from her body by exerting her will? And even though our card is motivated by genuine concern, the statement is, after all, a command. But we are commanding sick people to do something they can't do. If they could, they wouldn't be in the hospital. I don't know the origins of this strange statement, but my assumption is that it was intended to be understood passively. When we tell someone to get well, we are most likely not commanding him to exercise his volitional powers to make himself healthy. Instead, what we probably intend to communicate is something like this: "You are sick. I care about you and want you well. So please subject yourself to those things that ordinarily serve to fight off sickness. Eat your greens. Sleep to your heart's content. Take your vitamins. Get well!"

When Paul commands us to be transformed, He knows we have no ability to transform ourselves. Only the Spirit of Christ can make us like Christ. But like a sick person being told to "Get well soon," the church is being called on to subject itself to that which the Spirit uses to effect transformation—namely, His mind-renewing word. The humble pastor recognizes he has no ability to transform anyone. For "neither he who plants is anything, nor he who waters," but that does not discourage him from sowing the seed of the word and watering it because he knows that by this means God "gives the increase" (1 Cor. 3:7). Humble church members recognize how desperately they need the word, and so they possess an "aggressive attentiveness" to the reading and preaching of the Scriptures.[7] As the church humbly devotes itself to the prophetic and apostolic word, it is progressively transformed from one degree of humility to the next by the Spirit's power.

Nowhere does a church's devotion to God's mind-renewing word evidence itself more clearly than in public worship. Join a humble church for Sunday worship, and you will not encounter lighthearted skits or engaging cinematography. Instead, you will be confronted with the unvarnished, heart-searching word of Christ. Every element of worship will be governed by and suffused with His gospel. The sermon will not be a moralistic homily with a Scripture quotation tacked on. It will be an exposition of a particular text of the Scriptures, explaining, illustrating, and applying God's word to the hearers. The sacraments of baptism and the Lord's Supper will serve the word as tangible signs and seals, helping us to get our hands around God's truth. The prayers offered and the songs sung will be rooted in the Scriptures. Nothing in God's worship will be concocted by people. Humble worship is word-dependent, word-ordered, word-saturated, word-exalting worship.

God's lowly people are devoted to His book. "Give us the word!" is their ardent cry. If our churches desire to be the object of God's loving delight, this must be true of them. For, declares the Lord,

> On this one will I look:
> On him who is poor and of a contrite spirit,
> And who trembles at My word. (Isa. 66:2)

Lowly Supplication

Humble devotion to the word cannot be divorced from humble devotion to prayer. Just read Psalm 119. The psalmist's all-consuming affection for God's testimonies drives him to seek hard after God. Such impassioned, Spirit-filled praying, perhaps more than anything

---

7. The phrase "aggressive attentiveness" is taken from John Piper, *Reading the Bible Supernaturally: Seeing and Savoring the Glory of God in Scripture* (Wheaton, Ill.: Crossway, 2017), 325–37.

else, is the greatest indicator of humility. What is prayer but the church's expression of entire dependence on God and its pursuit of lasting satisfaction through loving communion with Him? Where prayer is wanting, humility is wanting. "Hardly anything," asserts Wayne Mack, "is more an evidence of pride than prayerlessness."[8] Where prayer is not prioritized and prized, self-sufficiency and self-wisdom are operative. Prayerlessness is pridefulness. It is God's children living under the delusion that they don't need the loving presence, provision, guidance, and protection of their Father.

The fiery British evangelist Leonard Ravenhill prophetically mourned in his day, "The Cinderella of the church today is the prayer meeting. This handmaid of the Lord is unloved and unwooed because she is not dripping with the pearls of intellectualism, nor glamorous with the silks of philosophy; neither is she enchanting with the tiara of psychology. She wears the homespuns of sincerity and humility and so is not afraid to kneel!"[9] Is it still the case that the prayer meeting is the church's Cinderella? Sadly, it appears to be. Our churches are ecstatic about programs and publications, but where is all the excitement for prayer? Our churches are devoted to a nearly endless frenzy of activity, but show me the church given to passionate prayer.

The early church devoted itself to corporate prayer (Acts 1:14; 2:42; 6:4). This was not a once-a-month, thirty-minute meeting that only 20 percent of the people attended. The household of God is a house of continual prayer. Paul commands the church on multiple occasions to be earnestly devoted to prayer:

- "Continuing steadfastly in prayer" (Rom. 12:12).
- "Praying always with all prayer and supplication in the Spirit, being watchful to this end with all perseverance and supplication for all the saints" (Eph. 6:18).
- "Continue earnestly in prayer, being vigilant in it with thanksgiving" (Col. 4:2).

---

8. Mack, *Humility: The Forgotten Virtue*, 48.
9. Leonard Ravenhill, *Why Revival Tarries* (Bloomington, Minn.: Bethany House, 1959), 19.

These are not suggestions or encouragements; they are commands directed to the corporate church in every age and in every place. God wants His people to give themselves to continual prayer with intense earnestness. This, of course, is not something we can conjure up. It is the fruit of God-fearing humility. God's house is a house of prayer because God's children recognize that apart from Him, they are nothing, have nothing, and can do nothing.

If you were to step into the pulpit from which I preach every Sunday, your eyes would immediately be drawn to a little white piece of paper taped to the top that reads, "APART FROM ME YOU CAN DO NOTHING." As I considered what I most needed to remember as a preacher, there seemed nothing more fundamental than this. I am utterly helpless apart from the Spirit of Christ. I cannot persuade anyone into the kingdom. I have no ability to make anyone in the room more holy by my eloquence or logical argumentation. I'm entirely cast on Christ because only He can do what needs to be done. That is humility's boast. Christ is all! And that is why the humble church is devoted to prayer.

Only Christ can raise a spiritually dead sinner to life and restore a broken marriage or a broken soul. Only Christ can effectively comfort the suffering or abused and make His people grow in spiritual maturity. Only Christ can extend the borders of the kingdom and deliver His church from the forces of darkness.

All our planning, programming, publishing, and promoting are in vain if they are void of the presence and power of Christ's Spirit. Do we actually believe that? The best way to find out is to look at our praying.

How much time do we set aside for corporate prayer? It is often claimed that quality is what matters, not quantity. But a careful look at the New Testament would reveal otherwise. Yes, the quality of our praying is of grave importance, but so also is the frequency of it. Devotion, constancy, steadfastness—these are the characteristics of the humble church's praying. "God's acquaintance is not made by quick visits," writes E. M. Bounds. "God does not bestow his gifts on the casual or hasty comers and goers."[10]

When we do pray corporately, what is the substance of our prayer to God? Many prayer meetings are dead because they consist of the mindless recitation of a laundry list of physical needs in the church. We certainly need to pray for these things (with our minds and hearts engaged). Our Father cares about all the minute details of our lives, and the humble look to Him in all things. But the lowly recognize that prayer is first and foremost about loving communion with their Father. They are less desirous of things from God and more desirous of God Himself. They draw near to their Creator through Christ. They relish in His beauty and glory. They praise Him for His goodness and grace. They confess their failings and sins. And they petition Him primarily not for physical blessings, but for spiritual blessings. They pray for God's name to be exalted and His kingdom to advance (Matt. 6:9–10). They pray for boldness and power to speak the word of Christ to a lost world (Acts 4:23–31). They pray for God to raise up laborers to proclaim His word to the four corners of the earth (Matt. 9:37–38). They pray for their persecuted brothers and sisters suffering for the faith (Heb. 13:3). They pray for the governing authorities over them, crying out for godly leaders and godly laws (1 Tim. 2:2). They pray for the illuminating work of the Spirit to open their eyes more and more to Christ and His love (Eph. 1:15–23; 3:14–19). They pray with intense longing for Christ to come again to consummate His kingdom (Rev. 22:20). The humble are not afraid to pray big prayers that could never be answered by anyone other than God, for the anthem of all their praying is, "Now to Him who is able to do exceedingly abundantly above all that we ask or think, according to the power that works in us, to Him be glory in the church by Christ Jesus to all generations, forever and ever. Amen" (Eph. 3:20–21).

The downward disposition of a Christward self-perception

---

10. *The Complete Works of E. M. Bounds on Prayer* (Grand Rapids: Baker Books, 1990), 460.

cannot help but pray like this. Pride—and pride alone—is the reason why corporate prayer is the Cinderella of our churches.

Lowly Ministration

The humble church will be a unified body, but such unity does not equal uniformity. Having stressed the oneness of the church (Eph. 4:4–6), the apostle clarifies, "But to each one of us grace was given according to the measure of Christ's gift" (v. 7). God's singular household is filled with children who have diverse personalities, levels of maturity, gifts, and roles. There is unity in diversity and diversity in unity.

It is the risen Christ who gifts His people in a multiplicity of ways. A gift is not something earned; it is something freely received. None of us get a say in how we are gifted or in the measure of giftedness we receive. Christ is the sovereign determiner and bestower of these abilities.

Sadly, Christ's gifts are often the playground of pride. As one who has a necessarily public gift, I understand this intimately. Every Lord's Day there is a war waging in my soul. Will I use my gift of preaching to exalt Christ or myself? It is incredibly easy to use my God-given gifts to proclaim a God-given gospel as a God-given messenger and to do it for the applause of people. There were men in Paul's day who were doing this, preaching the gospel "from selfish ambition" (Phil. 1:16). Regardless of the degree to which our gifts are public, we must take great care to use them as *gifts*. You don't boast in gifts. You give thanks and bless the giver. The healthy church is a body in which all the members are using Christ's gifts for Christ's glory.

But using your gift requires a proper self-perception: "For I say, through the grace given to me, to everyone who is among you, not to think of himself more highly than he ought to think, but to think soberly, as God has dealt to each one a measure of faith.… Having then gifts differing according to the grace that is given to us, let us use them" (Rom. 12:3, 6). To use our gifts in Christ's service, we must first come to terms with our particular giftedness. Nothing but our pride keeps us from such sober self-assessment. It does so in one of two ways:

1. Pride makes us think too highly of ourselves, claiming gifts and graces that have not actually been given to us or making us discontent with what Christ has given us under the guise that we deserve better.

2. Pride makes us think too lowly of ourselves (remember low self-esteem?), failing to exercise gifts Christ has given us out of sinful fear and insecurity.

Whether you think of yourself too highly or too lowly, you are thinking of yourself wrongly, and it is because you are failing to perceive yourself before Christ. To pridefully seek to use gifts we have not been given or to pridefully fail to use gifts that we have been given is detrimental to the life of the church.

Oh, how we need humility! This grace is what leads us to discover, cultivate, and use Christ's gifts in His service. Humility doesn't blush to assert, "God has gifted me to preach," or "God has gifted me in administration." We naturally assume such statements are prideful, but they are not prideful if we understand what a gift is. It is something we do not earn or deserve. So there is nothing to be proud about. To embrace and cultivate Christ's particular gifting is not arrogant; it is the proper response of understanding yourself before His glory.

Christ-Fearing Devotion

Everything set forth in this chapter could be summarized in two words: fear Christ. The downward disposition of humility is always wed to the upward disposition of loving fear. Such reverential, affectionate awe is what undergirds devotion. The humble are devoted to Christ in consecration, to His word in transformation, to His throne in supplication, and to His gifts in ministration just because their souls are placarded with His glory and beauty in the gospel. This is the glorious effect of humility—an all-consuming love for Christ that leads to an all-consuming devotion to Him in His church.

Are you a devoted member of a local church? The humble are.

◆ CHAPTER 11 ◆

Imperfect Members

My life is a constant reminder that I have not arrived. Take my drive home from work, for instance. I get into my car, weary from a stressful day. As I pull out of the church parking lot, I flip on a podcast featuring the day's news only to become gripped with anxiety over the uncertainty and turmoil in the world. Passing a chiropractic office, I begin to ponder my back problems and my need to improve my posture. In the self-same moment, some lady rudely cuts me off, resulting in murderous anger arising within. As I come to a stoplight, I see a homeless man holding a cardboard sign with a puppy at his side, and I critically think to myself, "If you are so broke that you cannot eat, how can you afford to care for a dog?" By the time I finally pull into the driveway, I'm praying, "Lord, I am physically and emotionally spent. I need your help to love Tessa and the boys tonight." And all of this within twenty minutes! If you are not being constantly reminded of your imperfect condition, it is only because you are living in a prideful slumber.

The congregation I serve is a part of the Orthodox Presbyterian Church (OPC for short). A joke that frequents our circles is that OPC stands for "Only Perfect Church." It is always said tongue in cheek, but I wonder at times if certain individuals actually believe it. That is what haughtiness does. It raises a person or a community beyond the ability of critique, and only perfection is beyond critique.

The reality, however, is that every local church and every denomination consists of a body of imperfect people. We have not yet arrived. The salvation we have already received in Christ is not yet complete. It is true that we will never be more loved or adopted than we already are in Christ. But there is a sense in which even our adoption is awaiting consummate finality: "for the earnest expectation of the creation eagerly waits for the revealing of the sons of God" (Rom. 8:19). And this leads us "who have the firstfruits of the Spirit" to "groan within ourselves, eagerly waiting for the adoption, the redemption of our body" (v. 23).

The present condition of adopted believers is one of struggle and sorrow. We are groaning for glory as we follow in the steps of our Savior. For "there is no consummate adoption," explains David Garner, "without first a suffering adoption; identifying fully with their Elder Brother, glorified sons are first suffering sons."[1] The crown is preceded by the crucible. But this crucible is gracious, coming from the loving heart of our heavenly Father. He uses the sin and the suffering in His house to drive His children downward.

Our Spiritual Imperfection

John Newton once described himself as "a heap of inconsistence."[2] This self-perception resonates with the inner contradiction I find in my own soul: "For the flesh lusts against the Spirit, and the Spirit against the flesh; and these are contrary to one another, so that you do not do the things that you wish" (Gal. 5:17). I genuinely want to please my Father. The Spirit of adoption graciously kindles such lowly longings within. But the flesh, that indwelling principle of arrogance, is always spoiling my attempts at loving and serving my Creator. I am a saint, but I am not perfectly sanctified.

---

1. David B. Garner, *Sons in the Son: The Riches and Reach of Adoption in Christ* (Phillipsburg, N.J.: P&R, 2016), 127.

2. John Newton, *The Works of John Newton* (Edinburgh: Banner of Truth, 1985), 6:98.

The paradox is that the more sanctified we become, the more unholy we sense ourselves to be. The lower we grow, the more haughtiness we perceive in our hearts. And as the light of Christ's glory progressively exposes our remaining corruption, it leads to lowly groaning.

A God-Inspired Groan

The apostle Paul gives vent to this in Romans 7:14–25. Here we are given the Bible's most detailed account of the adopted believer's struggle with indwelling sin.[3] Paul is looking at himself through the mirror of the Spirit-inspired law (v. 14). This is a Godward self-perception leading Paul, like Isaiah before him, to pronounce woe on himself:

- "I am carnal, sold under sin" (v. 14).
- "I know that in me (that is, in my flesh) nothing good dwells" (v. 18).
- "O wretched man that I am!" (v. 24).

His language is strong—so strong, in fact, that some doubt the man speaking is a Christian. He identifies himself with sin in verse 14 ("I am"), but then in the same breath he distinguishes himself from sin: "But now, it is no longer I who do it, but sin that dwells in me" (vv. 17, 20).

What are we to make of this? The apostle recognizes that the anti-God principle within is *his*. He can't point the finger and say, "God, it's not my fault! Blame it on the flesh." He takes responsibility for his sin and bemoans it. But he also recognizes that as one who is in Christ, he is not ultimately defined by sin. Pride is no longer the prevailing disposition of his heart and at the core of his identity. The sin dwelling in him is his sin, but it is not fundamental to his person. Only a Christward gaze can produce this delicate balance, and unfortunately it is quite rare in the church.

---

3. I am aware of the great exegetical difficulties this text presents and its various interpretations, but I remain convinced that the classic Augustinian view that Paul is speaking of his present experience as a man in Christ is the most compelling. See Sinclair B. Ferguson, *The Holy Spirit* (Downers Grove, Ill.: InterVarsity, 1996), 156–62.

Why We Don't Groan
As believers, we tend either to fail to grasp the depths of our remaining depravity, thinking we are awesome, or to become consumed with our remaining depravity, forgetting the awesomeness of God's grace. But the root of our blissful oblivion to the flesh and our obsessive fixation on the flesh is the same—a failure to eye Christ. When our gaze is not on our Creator and Redeemer, rest assured, it is set on the creature in some form or fashion.

In the context of the local church, such humanward pride often exercises itself by drawing comparisons between us and fellow church members. Instead of comparing ourselves to God with a steady faith in Christ, we compare ourselves to others with a steady faith in ourselves, leading to either presumption or pessimism.

- "Unlike the Xbox-playing so-and-so, I spend my free time reading John Calvin."
- "I know I should cut the porn, but at least I haven't had an affair like so-and-so."
- "If only I could be like so-and-so, who is so bold for Christ— but alas, I will never be comfortable sharing my faith."

Such prideful exaltation of the creature above the Creator keeps us from seeing the nature and extent of the problem in our souls. It also debilitates us by distracting us from Christ, whose beauty is the chief motivation and whose power is the sole impetus behind our war on sin. For when our hearts are filled with Christ, asks John Owen, "what access could sin, with its painted pleasures, with its sugared poisons, with its envenomed baits, have unto our souls?"[4]

The Humble Groan
Those who possess a Christward self-perception are not content with or debilitated by their present attainment of holiness. Instead, the

4. John Owen, *The Nature, Power, Deceit, and Prevalency of the Remainders of Indwelling Sin in Believers*, in *The Works of John Owen*, ed. William H. Goold (Edinburgh: Banner of Truth, 1966), 6:250.

humble are filled with a Christ-centered self-loathing. This sounds bleak and depressing to positive thinkers in the late modern era. But study church history and you will find that such lowly groaning has always been a characteristic mark of the most eminent saints. Take, for example, these sample entries from the diary of the American missionary David Brainerd:

- *April 1, 1742*: "Oh, that God would humble me deeply in the dust before Him! I deserve hell every day for not loving my Lord more, who has, I trust, loved me and given Himself for me. Every time I am enabled to exercise any grace renewedly, I am renewedly indebted to the God of all grace for special assistance.... Oh, if ever I get to heaven it will be because God wills, and nothing else; for I never did anything of myself but get away from God!"[5]

- *August 30, 1742*: "Oh, I saw what I owed to God in such a manner as I scarce ever did; I knew, I had never lived a moment to Him, as I should do. Indeed, it appeared to me I had never done anything in Christianity. My soul longed with a vehement desire to live to God."[6]

Do you hear the echoes of Romans 7? When was the last time you heard anyone talk like this? Why don't our journals express such grace-filled agonizing cries? It is because our soul gaze is not fixed on the Son of God who loved us and gave Himself for us.

Paul and Brainerd possessed low views of themselves not because their identity was rooted in the flesh, but because their identity was rooted in Christ. The more intimately acquainted they became with Him, the more they recognized how the flesh tainted even their best deeds. After all that God had done for them through the Mediator, they were still tirelessly prone to love and exalt the self. What reason for humble groaning! Octavius Winslow writes, "If there is one consideration more humbling than another to a spiritually-minded

---

5. *The Life and Diary of David Brainerd*, ed. Jonathan Edwards (Grand Rapids: Baker Books, 1989), 75.

6. *Life and Diary of David Brainerd*, 96.

believer, it is, that, after all God has done for him,—after all the rich displays of his grace, the patience and tenderness of his instructions, the repeated discipline of his covenant, the tokens of love received, and the lessons of experience learned, there should still exist in the heart a principle, the tendency of which is to secret, perpetual, and alarming departure from God."[7]

The Groaning Church

It is hard to imagine what an entire congregation composed of men, women, boys, and girls like Paul and Brainerd would look like. But is it too extreme to say that such ought to be the norm? I don't think so. A church growing downward in humility will consist of a group of members who are increasingly coming to terms with their sinful imperfections. This will produce a collective groaning that will bear many blessed fruits.

First, it will foster *loving unity* in the church. Humility causes us to see the blackness of our hearts in a way we couldn't possibly see in any other. Newton explains, "It is probable that all who are convinced and enlightened by the Holy Spirit, having a clearer knowledge of the nature, number, and aggravation of their own sins, than they can possibly have of those of any other person, account themselves among the chief of sinners, though many of them may have been preserved from gross enormities."[8] Members who "account themselves among the chief of sinners" are quick to overlook the faults and failings of others. They are amazed at Christ's lovingkindness toward them despite their continual pride, and this liberates them "to walk worthy of the calling with which [they] were called, with all lowliness and gentleness, with longsuffering, bearing with one another in love, endeavoring to keep the unity of the Spirit in the bond of peace" (Eph. 4:1–3).

Second, it will foster *loving submission* in the church. Christ governs the members of His church through elders who "watch out for [their] souls, as those who must give account" (Heb. 13:17). If you

---

7. Octavius Winslow, *Personal Declension and Revival of Religion in the Soul* (Edinburgh: Banner of Truth, 2021), 1.

8. Newton, *Works*, 5:173.

become a member of a church in my denomination, one of the questions you will be asked is, "Do you promise to participate faithfully in this church's worship and service, to submit in the Lord to its government, and to heed its discipline, even in case you should be found delinquent in doctrine or life?"[9] It is a sobering question, one that ought not to be answered flippantly. But for those who grasp their proneness to wander and their insane inclination toward deifying themselves, the answer is a no-brainer. They see God's fatherly kindness displayed in the gift of elders who hold them accountable, and they humbly submit (1 Peter 5:5). The humble praise Christ for instituting church discipline. They tremble at the thought of life without ecclesiastical accountability.

Third, it will foster *loving discipleship* in the church. The more we see our sin, the more we grow to hate it and long to be done with it. That is what led the apostle to cry, "O wretched man that I am! Who will deliver me from this body of death?" (Rom. 7:24). That is what led Brainerd to cry, "My soul longed with a vehement desire to live to God."[10] A church fueled by such restless hunger for holiness will be a church that takes discipleship seriously. Mature members will never tire of spurring one another onward toward greater conformity to Christ and will humbly come alongside the less mature members, helping them to grow by Christ's transforming Spirit and word.

To put it more simply, as we grow downward in humility, we grow outward in love. The humble recognition of what Westminster Confession 13.2 calls "a continual and irreconcilable war" between the flesh and the Spirit produces the self-giving fruit of love. Love is the lifeblood of a lowly spirit and of a lowly church.

God in His wisdom utilizes our remaining corruption to drive us lower, making us members who marvel at His love and demonstrate that love to every other member of the family, despite their present imperfections.

---

9. *The Book of Church Order of the Orthodox Presbyterian Church*, 2020 ed. (Willow Grove, Pa.: Orthodox Presbyterian Church, 2020), 158.

10. *Life and Diary of David Brainerd*, 96.

Our Physical Imperfection

A few months ago, I took off my shelf a book by J. I. Packer. For quite some time, I had thought it was entitled *Weakness in the Way*. It was a title that resonated with me. Weakness is an obstacle. Suffering is something to be overcome. Tribulations are a necessary evil that hinders us. But that day when I picked up the little volume, it suddenly dawned on me that I had been misreading the title the whole time. It was not *Weakness in the Way*; it was *Weakness Is the Way*.[11] This was a profound moment as God used my erroneous reading to expose my worldly thinking.

The world assures us that the elimination of weakness and the minimization of suffering are the paths to joy and life. Power is the way. Beauty is the way. Health is the way. Wealth is the way. Success is the way. But here was an entirely otherworldly way of thinking— weakness is the way. Where did Packer get such a strange notion? He got it from his Bible. Weakness is the way because humility is the way, and when God sanctifies our suffering, it produces a Christ-magnifying, lowly spirit in us.

We must not overlook God's sanctifying work. Not all suffering produces humility. Being diagnosed with terminal brain cancer does not automatically give you the downward disposition of a Christward self-perception. Living through the Great Depression or surviving Auschwitz will not necessarily make you humble. In fact, suffering has the potential to harden you in pride. It can, and often does, lead to creaturely fists raised in rebellion against God:

- "If God really loved me, He would not allow me to go through this."

- "God is either not good or nonexistent because He did absolutely nothing to stop the accident that took my husband and baby boy."

---

11. J. I. Packer, *Weakness Is the Way: Life with Christ Our Strength* (Wheaton, Ill.: Crossway, 2013).

Suffering, in all its devastating forms, can stoke the flames of devilish pride within. It is only suffering administered by the hand of the Spirit that leads to humility. I do not mean mere suffering, but *sanctified suffering*. This is suffering that drives us to Christ. The apostle Paul, once again, has much to teach us from his own personal experience.

Sanctified Suffering Frees Us from Self-Exaltation
Paul doesn't bother to give us details, but he tells us that God had afflicted him with "a thorn" in his physical body (2 Cor. 12:7). We might miss that God is the one doing this because Paul doesn't explicitly state it to be the case. But it becomes clear when he explains the reason behind this painful and undesirable affliction. Twice he says that it was given "lest I should be exalted above measure" (v. 7). Paul had received heavenly visions beyond our wildest imaginations, and this rich spiritual experience had the potential to puff him up with self-importance. So a sharp spike had been administered to keep him low. Satan was at work in this (he calls it "a messenger of Satan"), but clearly there was someone else giving it because Satan's great goal was to make Paul conceited, not deliver him from conceit. Paul's fatherly God was the one recognizing the threat of spiritual prosperity and afflicting His son to keep him from haughtiness.

It is in times of physical and spiritual prosperity, when God's providence smiles on us, that our hearts are, in the words of John Flavel, "exceeding apt to grow secure, proud, and earthly." He goes on to state that "a man humble under prosperity…is one of the greatest rarities in the world."[12] The proof for such a statement is not hard to find. Take a good look at your own heart. If you really grasp the potential for evil that remains in you, you will fear prosperity more than pain.

Pride in prosperity is what undergirded Israel's apostasy. Note God's rebuke of His covenant people:

I knew you in the wilderness,
In the land of great drought.

---

12. John Flavel, *Saint Indeed*, in *The Works of John Flavel* (Edinburgh: Banner of Truth, 1968), 5:437.

When they had pasture, they were filled;
They were filled and their heart was exalted;
Therefore they forgot Me. (Hos. 13:5–6)

That is a sobering summary of Israel's history, and it is precisely why God makes His new covenant people a suffering people. He knows our proneness to be lifted up with conceit (i.e., a haughty spirit) and to forget Him (i.e., a loss of a Godward self-perception). He mingles His fatherly blessings with afflictions to save us from ourselves.

Sanctified Suffering Frees Us from Self-Sufficiency

Paul pleaded for God to take away this thorn (2 Cor. 12:8). He didn't enjoy suffering, nor does he call us to. Suffering is always undesirable and unnatural. It is not the way the world was created to be. And that is why it produces groaning for deliverance. Sometimes God answers those groans by bringing relief in the here and now, but God did not remove Paul's cross, just as He did not remove the cross of Paul's Savior. Instead, He declared, "My grace is sufficient for you, for My strength is made perfect in weakness" (v. 9). Paul had prayed persistently for God to remove it. But God responded, "No, My son. I have something far better to give you than the removal of this affliction—My all-sufficient grace!"

God's providential thorns, whether they come in the form of chronic pain, job loss, the death of a loved one, relational distress, terminal illness, or any host of day-to-day trials, are messengers from God reminding us of our weakness and frailty. In His lovingkindness our Father uses suffering to deliver us from our arrogant tendency to depend on our own resources. But He doesn't merely want us to know our weakness. He wants us to know His strength. He tailors afflictions, big and small, for every child in His family to drive them out of themselves to Christ. Weakness is the way because weakness leads us by the hand to Christ's strength. It produces a Christward self-perception: "Therefore most gladly I will rather boast in my infirmities, that the power of Christ may rest upon me" (2 Cor. 12:9).

When suffering is sanctified to a church, it will cease boasting in its accomplishments or attainments or experiences or abilities.

It will begin to boast in those things that make it weak because it recognizes that Christ's resurrection power is manifested through the cross. Such a church is not interested in showing the world its strength. It longs for Christ's mighty arm to be manifested, and so it embraces its physical, psychological, and economical weaknesses, casting itself on its elder Brother to do what only He can.

Sanctified Suffering Frees Us from Self-Sagacity
You may be thinking to yourself, "That all sounds nice, but there has to be a better way to make us humble and dependent. Do we really have to suffer?"

That question never crossed the apostle's mind. Suffering was assumed, and Paul was content. Weaknesses, insults, hardships, persecutions, calamities—he was content with them all (2 Cor. 12:10).

Discontentment arises when we think we know better than God. It arises when I get a flat tire and declare in anger that my day has been wasted. I had plans to be eminently productive that day, but God had other plans. His plans were for me to spend the bulk of my time at the auto shop, forking out a couple hundred dollars for a tow and a tire. Discontentment arises when I think, "No, God, this should not be happening right now." It arises when I consider myself as the sage, as the source of wisdom and truth. It arises when I am wise in my own eyes. But the more we see our fatherly God using suffering to deliver us from self-exaltation and self-sufficiency, the more content we become. We begin to grasp that we don't know best; God does. He knows the best means to bring about the best ends. He knows what would become of His children if their lives were filled with unabated prosperity, comfort, and ease.

I have had poor posture for as long as I can remember. I'm a perpetual sloucher. A few months ago, I began to come to terms with the reality that if I don't do something about it, I am going to face debilitating back and neck problems in the future. So I've been getting adjusted by a local chiropractor. There are days when he gives me a hard and painful crack. But never once have I yelled, "Hey, you idiot! Stop being so rough!" I don't know how to fix my posture. He is the one who has devoted his life to studying the spine. He is the sage. And I submit to his wisdom in the chiropractic realm and am willing to endure the pain he deems necessary because I trust he knows far better how to fix me than I do. If I am willing to submit to a fallible creature to change my physical posture, how much more ought I to willingly look to my infallible Father to change my prideful posture? He knows the best way to do it, and often it is painful.

Scripture speaks with one voice to the church—suffering is our lot in the here and now. It ought not to surprise us, for it is the tool God uses to shape His children into a humble community that depends entirely on His strength. Have you ever wondered why the church flourishes and advances in times of great persecution? It is because when God sanctifies these trials, it produces a people who have the downward disposition of a Christward self-perception.

Owning Our Imperfections

Take a good look at the members of your church this coming Lord's Day. Beneath his clean-shaven, Sunday-best appearance is a wretched, prideful disease, seeking to undo the Spirit's humbling work. Behind her wide grin is a pain and grief that words cannot express. How quick we are to forget this! How quick we are to pridefully give the appearance that we have it all together! This keeps us from being able to love and minister to one another as God desires us to.

In this life God's children are imperfect family members. They are fraught with imperfections. But that is the point. These sinners and sufferers have been gathered not because of their perfection or strength, but because of Christ's. And every imperfection in both body and soul is intended to press them ever lower before His flawless majesty and ever outward in loving service to one another.

◆ CHAPTER 12 ◆

Missional Members

Evangelism. If you are anything like me, the word has the remarkable ability to make you cringe. It can produce mixed emotions and unhappy thoughts. It can cause the palms to sweat and a list of excuses to arise. It is safe to assume that few readers squealed with delight at reading this word. Why?

Our cringing may be the result of seeing evangelism abused (e.g., the angry street preacher yelling, "God hates you!"). Our cringing may be the result of a narrow-minded view of evangelism (e.g., "I must be out on the street, passing out tracks and doing open-air preaching"). But in many cases, our cringing is symptomatic of self-serving pride.

Evangelism is uncomfortable. It is telling a world that is not humble about the humble Christ. To proclaim this message is to meet with hostility because people who lack humility aren't very fond of being called to bow as sinners before the absolute, undiluted lordship of Jesus Christ. Given our fallen context, evangelism is cross-shaped, and crosses make us cringe. But if the church would follow its Master, it must embrace this cross with joy.

Only the humble, seeing themselves before Christ's mediatorial glory, can do that. Like humility, evangelizing is first and foremost about identity, not activity. The King of the universe doesn't merely call us to the act of witnessing; He calls us to *be* His witnesses.[1] That is an incredible thought! Those whom Christ represents before God are called to represent Him before the world. The humble glory in such a call, taking up their cross and following their Master. They are missional members of "loving communities committed to sharing the gospel as part of an ongoing way of life."[2]

The Humble Aim of a Missional Church

As a pastor, I understand that arm-twisting, guilt trips, and threats are not effective ways to orient the members of my church toward mission. Kingdom witness must come from a genuine desire to see the lost found and the reign of Christ extended. But for many of us, such desire, while not entirely absent, is shamefully lacking. What is the cause of our apathy toward a lost world?

The answer is simple. We are proud. The Christ-glorifying, people-loving motives that ought to drive us to witness are deficient because humility is deficient.

Driven to Mission by Love for Souls

Romans 9 is one of the most difficult chapters in Scripture to come to terms with. Paul's teaching on God's exhaustive and unconditional sovereignty in salvation is not what makes it a difficult pill to swallow, for that is simply what it means for God to be God. What causes problems for me are the opening verses: "I tell the truth in Christ, I am not lying, my conscience also bearing me witness in the Holy Spirit, that I have great sorrow and continual grief in my heart. For I could wish that I myself were accursed from Christ for my brethren, my countrymen according to the flesh" (vv. 1–3). I have a category for a sovereign God, but I don't have a category for this kind of excruciating, continual, tormenting anguish over the lost.

---

1. Rebecca Manley Pippert, *Stay Salt: The World Has Changed, Our Message Must Not* (Epsom, England: Good Book Company, 2020), 68.

2. J. Mack Stiles, *Evangelism: How the Whole Church Speaks of Jesus* (Wheaton, Ill.: Crossway, 2014), 47.

I'm tempted to think Paul was getting a little carried away, exaggerating about how he really felt. But, as if being an inspired apostle was not enough, he goes out of his way to stress the truthfulness of his claim.

I can count on only one hand the number of times I have shed a tear for the lost. The constancy and intensity of this apostolic anguish is altogether foreign to me. I just don't love people like Paul does. And it is, in part, because I don't see people like Paul does.

The path from pride to humility not only entails a reformation of our self-perception but also a reformation of our perception of others. The downward disposition of humility changes how we view every person on the planet. As I search my own heart, one thing that becomes immediately apparent is that I have the tendency to perceive people as people-in-themselves. The teller at the bank is *merely* a person. The mother of three at the grocery store is *merely* a person. The widow who lives across the street is *merely* a person. I tend to espouse worldly ways of categorizing people (e.g., rich or poor, dorky or cool). In my pride I fail to see others as image-bearing creatures in a covenant relationship with their Creator. I fail to perceive them as either helplessly lost in Adam or gloriously saved in Christ. People are just people. This is a primary reason why my heart doesn't break like the apostle's.

If people are not image-bearing creatures who possess inherent worth and dignity, then what reason is there for me to care about them? If people are not corrupt creatures who are helplessly hellbound, then what reason is there for sorrowing over them? If people are *merely* people, then Paul's anguish is the height of lunacy. But what the school of humility teaches us is that every person we encounter is fundamentally related to God, either in Adam or in Christ. It enables us to properly see others, causing us to love them. To the degree we truly understand that our unsaved family members, coworkers, neighbors, and friends are covenantal creatures who are desperately corrupt and desperately in need of a Mediator, we will be moved with compassion. Such a vision will drive us to weep. It will drive us to pray. It will drive us to witness. It will drive us to pick up our souls with Samuel Davies and cry,

> Why does not my heart always glow with affection and zeal for them! Oh! Why am I such a languid friend when the love of my Master and his Father is so ardent! When the ministers of heaven are flaming fires of love, though they do not share in the same nature! And when the object of my love is so precious and valuable!...Oh! shall not I love them! Shall not love invigorate my hand, to pluck them out of the burning! Yes, I will, I must love them. But, ah! To love them more! Glow, my zeal! kindle, my affections! speak, my tongue! flow, my blood! be exerted, all my powers! be, my life! if necessary, a sacrifice to save souls from death![3]

Driven to Mission by Love for Christ

Humility, as we have seen, is all about a loving relationship with the triune God. It is the proper disposition of those who live in His loving presence. Thus, it is always wed to a loving fear of God. It is produced by a Godward or Christward gaze. The church fully fixated on Christ will possess a volcano-like passion for Christ's redeeming beauty to be known and adored throughout the earth.

When the exalted Christ began His new covenant mission by pouring out His Spirit on the day of Pentecost (Acts 2:1–13), the end goal was worship. This becomes especially clear when read in light of the early chapters of Genesis. God had commissioned both Adam and Noah to be fruitful, multiply, and fill the earth with image-bearing worshipers (Gen. 1:28; 9:1). But in their pride, they failed to carry out this commission, and this failure came to a head at Babel. Up to this point, humanity had a singular language (11:1). But instead of uniting to spread God's worship around the globe, they came together, saying, "Let us make a name for ourselves, lest we be

---

3. Samuel Davies, "The Love of Souls, a Necessary Qualification for the Ministerial Office," in *Sermons of the Rev. Samuel Davies* (Morgan, Pa.: Soli Deo Gloria, 1995), 3:518.

scattered abroad over the face of the whole earth" (v. 4). These arrogant people rejected the creation mandate and built what we know as the Tower of Babel. It was humankind's attempt to exalt themselves. And it resulted in God coming down in judgment, confusing their languages, and scattering their persons. But on the day of Pentecost, Christ's Spirit was poured out to graciously reverse Babel.[4] The contrasts are striking:

- Babel was about proud men attempting to ascend to heaven; Pentecost was about the humble Christ descending from heaven by His Spirit.

- Babel resulted in confusion and misunderstanding of language; Pentecost resulted in clarity and understanding of language.

- Babel resulted in a united people being scattered and divided; Pentecost resulted in a divided people being gathered and united.

But the foremost contrast is one of worship. The purpose of Babel was the worship of humankind. The purpose of Pentecost was the worship of Christ. Christ was empowering His new covenant church to speak the gospel with the goal of transforming human-worshiping Babel into a Christ-worshiping church. He was fulfilling the original creation mandate as the second Adam, beginning to restore His image bearers throughout the earth for His glory and praise.[5]

John Piper contends that "worship is the fuel and goal of missions."[6] Missions results when Christ fearers, driven by faith-filled delight in Christ ("the fuel"), make it their ambition to spread His happy fear in the earth ("the goal"). Only the humble know this exulting in Christ that fires a passion for others to exult in Him.

---

4. Dennis E. Johnson, *The Message of Acts in the History of Redemption* (Phillipsburg, N.J.: P&R, 1997), 60.

5. John M. Frame, *The Doctrine of the Christian Life* (Phillipsburg, N.J.: P&R, 2008), 310.

6. John Piper, *Let the Nations Be Glad! The Supremacy of God in Missions*, 3rd ed. (Grand Rapids: Baker Academic, 2010), 15.

The proud church says, "Let us make a name for ourselves!" But the humble church says, "Let us live to magnify the name of the Lord in our community and world!" The measure of our evangelistic zeal is one telling mark of how much we truly fear Christ and, therefore, of how humble we truly are.

Not Two Drives, but One
Which drive ought to have the preeminence—love for souls or love for Christ? The Scriptures challenge such questions. There is only one predominant motivation for missions, but that motive can be viewed from two perspectives, the one focused on creatures (loving concern) and the other on the Creator (loving fear). The great drive of missions is the worship of the Creator, which simultaneously brings the Creator glory and the creature satisfaction.[7] The worship of God and the salvation of man are not two different pursuits.

Missional members long for Christ's saving might to be manifest among all the nations so that all peoples might be ushered into the joyous exultation of God (Psalm 67). When we see ourselves and others in the light of Christ's kingly glory, love for souls and love for Christ become so inseparably wed that they are one.

Without this humble drive, you will never be a missional church member. Without this humble drive, your congregation will never be a missional church.

The Humble Courage of a Missional Church
When I was in my early twenties, I worked at a family-owned butcher shop. God taught me a number of profound lessons there, but one stands out in particular. A fellow employee, Julia, was heading off to college, and we were all lined up to say goodbye. Being the introvert that I am, I was internally processing my last words to Julia as I waited my turn. My mind quickly ran through the usual "Christian" forms of goodbye:

---

7. For more on this, you can pick up or listen to just about anything from John Piper. *Let the Nations Be Glad!* is a great place to start.

- "God bless you, Julia." This seemed cliché.
- "God be with you, Julia." This seemed awkward.
- "I'll be praying for you, Julia." This seemed dishonest.

So what would I say? Here were my final words to Julia: "Good luck." Now that is a culturally acceptable statement, but it is not a biblically sound statement. I knew that to be the case, but in the moment, I chose to play the hypocrite. I didn't believe in luck. My worldview left nothing to chance. But as I said goodbye, I set aside my Christian convictions out of a desire to appear normal. Why? Because I feared what Julia and others would think of me.

I guarantee that no one from the butcher shop remembers my words that day, but I do because God graciously used my playacting hypocrisy to cut me deep. I was, and continue to be, a man fearer. William Perkins speaks of the Christian soul as a mixture of fears wherein "the fear of God is joined with the corrupt fear of man. And in this mixture sometimes the one prevails; sometimes, the other."[8] On that day, corrupt fear prevailed within, and it led to corrupt lips.

Evangelism and the Fear of People

As the West becomes increasingly secularized, the temptation is to fear. It is always the temptation the church faces as it lives in a hostile world. And where this creature-centered fear prevails, the church's mission is forfeited.

What is it that most prevents us from sharing our faith? What is it that keeps us silent when we know we should speak? What is it that leads us to conform to the world's standards and play the hypocrite? Sinful fear. When it comes to evangelism, here are some of my fears:

- I fear being looked down on as an irrational fool or completely rejected as a narrow-minded bigot.
- I fear being physically threatened or harmed.

---

8. William Perkins, *Commentary on Galatians*, in *The Works of William Perkins*, vol. 2, ed. Paul M. Smalley (Grand Rapids: Reformation Heritage Books, 2015), 104.

- I fear communicating the message wrongly or failing to have answers to the nearly unending number of possible objections that could be raised.
- I fear manipulating someone into professing faith prematurely.

Did you catch the similarity among all these fears? It is the one letter pronoun *I*. There is an idolatrous fixation on the self. The fear of people, which keeps my lips from speaking the gospel, flows from a haughty heart that is preoccupied with me, myself, and I: self-promotion, self-preservation, self-wisdom, self-reliance.

I don't evangelize because I fear people, and I fear people because I am proud. Take a good look at your own heart, and I guarantee you will find the same. The vestiges of pride are within us all, producing creature-exalting fears. And nothing presents more of a roadblock to God's children embracing God's mission than this.[9]

Do You Fear People or Love Them?

We fear people and do not speak because our perception of ourselves is not Christward. We're not basking in Christ's love. We're not zealous for His glory and longing for His smile. We're not eyeing His promises and precepts. The self has overshadowed the Christ. But there is more going on here than this. Not only have we misperceived ourselves, but our vision of others has been distorted by our Christ-belittling arrogance. We are afraid because we have elevated people above the God-man. We see them as more powerful than He is. We see them as more in control than He is. We see them as wiser than He is. We forget that the people we encounter are morally accountable, entirely dependent, radically corrupt creatures who will give an account to Christ. We forget that they cannot speak a word, think a thought, or lift a finger apart from His will. In short, we exalt the creature above the Creator.

---

9. J. Mack Stiles, "What If I'm Not a Gifted Evangelist?," Christian Living, The Gospel Coalition, January 31, 2011, https://www.thegospelcoalition.org /article/what-if-im-not-a-gifted-evangelist/.

We have already seen that this is the problem undergirding our lack of love toward other people. In our pride, we misperceive people and thus fail to affectionately seek after their eternal good. Our deficiency in love toward a lost world is not unrelated to our sinful fear toward a lost world. Both are the result of viewing people as people-in-themselves. Where deficiency in love is present, sinful fear is present.

If we fear people, we cannot love them, for our fear is the result of idolizing people. "We worship them," writes Ed Welch, "hoping they will take care of us, hoping they will give us what we feel we need."[10] People become a means to fulfilling and satisfying us. They become a tool that we seek to manipulate so they will praise us. But love does not view people as means to obtaining self-serving ends; love treasures its object as an end in itself. It is a treasuring affection that so values its object that it leads to selfless, sacrificial acts in the pursuit of the object's good. So long as we fear people, we will not love them. Is this perhaps why we are strangers to the unceasing, heart-piercing desire of the apostle to see sinners saved?

We need to examine ourselves at this point. Wherever we discover the fear of people lurking, we must pick it up by the throat and slay it. That is where humility comes in. Contrary to popular thought, humility is not a timid, easygoing pushover. Humility is ruthless in the cause of God and against the fear of people.

Replace Your Fear with Fear
Humility turns our gaze to the exalted Christ to whom "all authority has been given…in heaven and on earth" (Matt. 28:18). It sets apart Christ as Lord in the heart (1 Peter 3:15). It fears "Him who is able to destroy both soul and body in hell" (Matt. 10:28).

The Christward self-perception of humility sets straight our souls. Our pride exalts the creature, but humility exalts the Creator.

---

10. Edward T. Welch, *When People Are Big and God Is Small: Overcoming Peer Pressure, Codependency, and the Fear of Man* (Phillipsburg, N.J.: P&R, 1997), 182.

Our pride links arms with the fear of people, but humility links arms with the fear of Christ. And that is the only way to overcome our sinful fears! Arrogant people-fear can only be mortified by humble God-fear. John Flavel states, "The fear of God will swallow up the fear of man, a reverential awe and dread of God will extinguish the slavish fear of the creature, as the sun-shine puts out fire, or as one fire fetches out another; so will this fear fetch out that."[11]

Unlike the unloving fear of people, the fear of God is a loving fear. It is a tenderly affectionate fear that delights in the Lord above all else. And it frees us to love fellow creatures. It liberates us "to need them *less* and love them *more.*"[12] In so doing, it emboldens us amid a hostile world. Pride is what makes us wimpy, not humility. The downward disposition of a Christward self-perception clads our hearts with supernatural courage to fulfill Christ's mission for His glory and the eternal good of others. It makes us willing to have our reputations marred, our comforts withheld, our intelligence mocked, and our safety violated because it is no longer about us.

The Humble Message of a Missional Church

Humility recalibrates our souls to love Christ and people, which propels us to witness. But what is it that we bear witness to? In a real sense, we bear witness to the humble truths we have encountered up to this point.

- We tell people they are image-bearing creatures who are entirely dependent on God for their life, identity, and satisfaction (chapter 1).

- We impress on them that they are not the definers of the moral order, but that they are morally and covenantally accountable to their Creator (chapter 2).

- We seek to show them their finitude and fallibility in the light of the infinitude and infallibility of their Maker (chapter 3).

---

11. John Flavel, *A Practical Treatise of Fear*, in *The Works of John Flavel* (Edinburgh: Banner of Truth, 1968), 3:244.

12. Welch, *When People Are Big and God Is Small*, 19.

- We proclaim the holiness of God and the devastating rebellion of all people (chapter 4).

- We call out their delusional condition for what it is so that they might come to their senses (chapter 5).

- We extol the justice of God and their utter helplessness to pay their sinful debt or liberate themselves from their sinful bondage (chapter 6).

- We labor with all of our might to placard the God-man before them in His perfect life and sacrificial death, calling them to repentance and faith (chapter 7).

- We tell them with awe on our lips of the love of God for sinners, pleading with them not to reject this infinite ocean of divine affection (chapter 8).

- We seek to set forth Christ clothed in His multiplicity of saving benefits—a whole Savior for the whole person (chapter 9).

- We call them not only to repentance and faith but also to the waters of baptism, to be added to the Christ-worshiping church (chapter 10).

- We do not trifle with the lies of prosperity preachers but inform our hearers that to follow Christ entails a cross now (chapter 11).

If our mission is about making proud idolaters into humble worshipers, then it ought to be no surprise that our message is pervaded with Christ-magnifying humility. The more mastered you are by these truths, the more ready you will be to share your faith, for the downward disposition of a Christward self-perception is the essence of your call to a lost world.

Humility not only gives shape to the substance of our message but also to the delivery of that message. Here is how Peter puts it: "'Do not be afraid of their threats, nor be troubled.' But sanctify the Lord God in your hearts, and always be ready to give a defense to everyone who asks you a reason for the hope that is in you, with meekness and fear" (1 Peter 3:14–15). He is calling us to a Christ-fearing readiness to speak the gospel, clarifying that it must be done in a posture of humility, "with meekness and fear [i.e., respect]."

Pride doesn't just have the potential to prevent our witness; it has the potential to pervert our witness. Our speaking may quickly become about winning an argument or proving our intellectual superiority. We might get overly defensive, resorting to unkind and strong speech to silence our opponents. Or—less pertinent to Peter's focus but very relevant for us—we might evangelize so we can go boast about it to other Christians.

Prideful evangelism! We have all seen it. And only the Christ we proclaim can save us from it. To proclaim Christ with anything less than the downward disposition of a Christward self-perception is to be a living contradiction of the very realities your lips are uttering. Humility is the need of the hour.

Missional Is Not Optional

Two centuries ago Alexander Duff warned, "What is the whole history of the Christian Church, but one perpetual proof and illustration of the grand position—that an evangelistic or missionary church is a spiritually flourishing church; and, that a church which drops the evangelistic or missionary character, speedily lapses into superannuation [inability to serve due to old age] and decay."[13] We would do well to pause and consider these words. The church void of missional members is, at best, dying and may even be dead.

There is no one-size-fits-all when it comes to evangelism. All churches and church members have to wrestle with their unique gifts, personalities, and opportunities. But if you are a member of Christ's body, being missional is not optional. The humble understand this. Delivered from cowardly pride, they are passionate for Christ and souls. Delivered from delusional lies, they are schooled in the gospel they are called to proclaim. They cannot help but speak of Him who has loved them so (Acts 4:20).

---

13. Alexander Duff, *Missions: The Chief End of the Christian Church* (Edinburgh: J. Johnstone, 1839), 15.

PART 5

Eschatological Humility

eschatological: pertaining to the last things or end times
We are grave-bound, judgment-bound, and eternity-bound mortals.

CHAPTER 13

Grave-Bound Mortals

Last week I received the tragic news that my grandpa's best friend of seventy-nine years had died. He and his wife had left the house for an ice cream cone, but they never made it to Dairy Queen, and they never made it home. While they were waiting at a red light, a woman driving full speed rear-ended them. The impact caused their vehicle to fly off the road and into a tree. They were killed instantly.

Death is something all of us must face but none of us want to talk about. When we hear tragic stories like that of my grandpa's friend, our hearts go out to the families and loved ones affected. But then we quickly attempt to dismiss the fact that death is coming for us too, and there is no telling when or where or how. The death rate of the human race is not 97.4 percent. It is not as though there is a high likelihood of death but a chance we might be spared. Yet we have the uncanny tendency to believe such is the case with reference to ourselves. We would, of course, never put it in such stark terms. But it is the unspoken, often even unreasoned response of our hearts, shunning the bleak reality that the grave is coming for *us*. Others may die unexpectedly and suddenly in car accidents, but that could not happen to us on our drive to work tomorrow or on next month's family vacation.

Pride, as we have seen, lives in unrealities. It feeds off an unrealistic view of the self. One such unreality is a self-perceived immortality. All of us will die. We are mortals. But pride is preoccupied with convincing us otherwise. And that is because few realities strike a blow to our arrogance like the grave. The deified self is cut down to size at the cemetery.

We need to turn our attention to the future as we apply the final strokes of the brush to our portrait of a Godward self-perception. Eschatology, the doctrine of the last things, has classically concentrated on three dominant future realities: the grave, the judgment, and the eternal state. These coming realities will preoccupy our attention for the remainder of the book, and we begin here with the first—the grave.

The Grave Is a School in Creatureliness

The Scriptures have much to say about death, but the prayer of Moses in Psalm 90 is perhaps the most eloquent and experiential exposition of the grave ever penned. Here we find the well-known petition "Teach us to number our days, that we may gain a heart of wisdom" (v. 12). What Moses impresses on us throughout the psalm is that living in light of our grave (that is what it means "to number our days") is simply what the humble do. It is the result of the downward disposition of a Godward self-perception. That is why Moses begins with God:

> Lord, You have been our dwelling place in all generations.
> Before the mountains were brought forth,
> Or ever You had formed the earth and the world,
> Even from everlasting to everlasting, You are God." (vv. 1–2)

Before the invention of the automobile and the cultural breakdown of the family, the same house would often be the residence of generation after generation. The longest-standing wooden structure in America is a house built in the early 1640s for the Fairbanks family. Over the course of 268 years, eight generations of Fairbanks lived in this house. Today the home is a museum-like relic, but Moses is setting forth God as the dwelling place of His people not for a mere eight generations, but for all generations. Such is possible only because He is the everlasting Creator. He is not bound by time. He is not here today and gone tomorrow. He is eternal. Generations come and generations go, but God is the constant, never-dying refuge of His beloved children.

Moses cannot consider God in His eternality without considering his own mortality. We discussed God's eternality in relation to our creaturely temporality in chapter 3, but this vision of God's timeless majesty takes us by the hand to the grave. Speaking to the eternal One, Moses declares, "You return man to dust and say, 'Return, O children of man!'" (Ps. 90:3 ESV). If death teaches us anything, it is that we are not in control. We don't determine our death any more than we determine our birth. The God who formed us from the dust is the one who returns us to the dust. He is the sovereign numberer of our days (139:16). When He commands, "Return!" our bodies take their place among the generations of image-bearing dust that have gone before us. And here is a sobering reality: we don't get a say in when that command comes. It could come at any moment.

The congregation I pastor pays for me to have life insurance. But I have never actually gotten it. I intend to eventually, but it just seems like a waste of money now. I'm young, perfectly healthy (as far as I can tell), and have my whole life ahead of me. Maybe in twenty years I'll consider life insurance, but not now.

Do you see what I have done? I have subtly convinced myself that I'm not dying. Other thirty-year-olds die in plane crashes, get terminal cancer, and are killed in drive-by shootings. But that would never happen to me!

I live under the assumption that death, at least in this moment, cannot touch me. It is a wrong assumption. It is a misperception of me. It is a failure to reckon with the fact that my life is a vapor, here for a moment and then quickly vanishing (James 4:13–14). It is a godless vision, keeping me from the truth that at any moment, even as I type these words in the comfort of my study, my fatherly Creator could say, "Return, O son of man!" and I would drop down cold. It is pride, not good stewardship, that keeps me from opening a life insurance policy. "Death may be coming but not anytime soon," is what the arrogant tell themselves. But creatures like us are always traveling to the grave, and many of us are far closer than we realize.[1] We are not in control. We are not the Creator.

The Grave Is a School in Corruption

Our death, then, is intended to promote within us a controlling sense of our creatureliness, but it likewise promotes a controlling sense of our corruption. Look again at Psalm 90:3 (ESV): "You return man to dust and say, 'Return, O children of man!'" Did you notice the clear reference to Genesis 3? Adam's covenant-breaking led to covenant curse, and part of that curse was, "for dust you are, and to dust you shall return" (Gen. 3:19). Moses is grappling with God's curse on our sin. God's command is better translated, "Return, O children of Adam!" Adam's sin resulted in death not merely for himself but for all his posterity.[2] For "through one man sin entered the world, and death through sin, and thus death spread to all men" (Rom. 5:12). Death is not the inevitable end of mere creatures; death is the inevitable end of corrupt creatures.

Moses understands that death is penal. It is the just penalty of our sin (Rom. 6:23).

> For we have been consumed by Your anger,
> And by Your wrath we are terrified.
> You have set our iniquities before You,
> Our secret sins in the light of Your countenance.
> (Ps. 90:7–8)

The reason the death rate is 100 percent is because the sin rate is 100 percent. The grave schools us in our native corruption and our

---

1. I'm reminded of two preachers of old, David Brainerd and Robert Murray M'Cheyne. Do you know how old each of them lived to be? Twenty-nine. Or consider the beloved missionary to Ecuador, Jim Elliot. He died at the ripe old age of twenty-eight. Death is no respecter of ministerial usefulness or age.

2. This death was not merely spiritual but also physical. Before the fall, physical death could not touch God's image. See Leon Morris, *The Wages of Sin* (London: Tyndale, 1955), 10.

Creator's holy justice. Every funeral is a distressing lesson in the sinfulness of sin.

We live in an age, however, that seeks with all its might to dress up death. The modern funeral industry rakes in millions of dollars making death appear natural and pleasant. The dead are placed in beautiful, velvet-decked caskets dressed in fancier clothes than they ever wore during their lifetime, covered in makeup to disguise their lifeless complexion, and made to have positive expressions on their faces. It is humankind's best attempt at making death appear less than death.[3]

Death is horrible. It is unnatural and unpleasant. It informs us that something is terribly wrong with our world. It impresses on us what we are determined in our pride to suppress—namely, that we are morally accountable, covenantal creatures who have rebelled. Every death proclaims the universal fallenness of humankind. Our prideful effort to beautify the dead is an attempt to avoid the living God.

You are dying. So am I. We are grave-bound mortals. Why? Because of sin. The grave is the ever-present reminder of our prideful condition.

The Grave Is a School in Humble Wisdom

One of my all-time favorite films is *A Hidden Life*, based on the true story of an Austrian farmer named Franz Jägerstätter. Out of religious conviction, he refused to support Hitler's regime, leading to his imprisonment and eventual execution. What makes the film so powerful is its realism. There is no happy ending. There is no sudden rescue at the last moment. Death in its most brutal form is the taste left in your mouth. The final scene shows a widowed mother of young children. It is true to life, unlike the romanticized anti-realism of so many modern productions.[4]

---

3. Matthew McCullough, *Remember Death: The Surprising Path to Living Hope* (Wheaton, Ill.: Crossway, 2018), 40–43.

4. Carl Trueman expresses his own frustration in this regard: "I remember my jaw hitting the floor some years ago when I watched a Disney version of

Humility prizes reality, which is why Moses prays, "So teach us to number our days, that we may gain a heart of wisdom" (Ps. 90:12). His Godward gaze has confronted him with his mortality as a corrupt creature. And he doesn't want to lose this sense. He knows that his soul is ever attempting to live in unrealities and that only God can keep him from living in a fairytale dreamland. So he prays for help to live in the conscious orbit of his fast-approaching funeral. That sounds pessimistic to the proud. But the humble know it is realism of the profoundest sort, leading to wisdom. How can a preoccupation with death produce wisdom? There are at least two ways revealed in the graveside petitions of Moses.

First, a humble reckoning with our own death confronts us with the fleetingness of creaturely applause. Fools seek their worth in the favor of others. They are consumed with what other creatures think of them. They live for the respect and esteem of their peers and superiors. But the grave makes us wise by showing us that all creaturely praise will die with the creature. It leads the humble to seek after the only favor that lasts beyond the grave, that of the Creator.

> Return, O Lord! How long?
>   Have pity on your servants!
> Satisfy us in the morning with your steadfast love,
>   that we may rejoice and be glad all our days.
> (Ps. 90:13–14 ESV)

What is the fleeting love of people compared with the eternal love of God? "Everything in this life is going to be taken away from us," writes Tim Keller, "except one thing: God's love, which can go into death with us and take us through it and into His arms. It's the one thing you can't lose."[5] The grave is causing Moses to seek after

---

Notre Dame de Paris where the Hunchback does not die but lives happily ever after.... The point of the story of Quasimodo is that the guy with the hump dies at the end, and it's all terribly sad. My wife is meant to cry, and I am meant to feel angry at the raw deal Quasimodo has been dealt in the poker game of life." *Fools Rush in Where Monkeys Fear to Tread: Taking Aim at Everyone* (Phillipsburg, N.J.: P&R, 2012), 169–70.

5. Timothy Keller, *On Death* (New York: Penguin, 2020), 26.

the eternal affection of His covenant God in the here and now. He is humbly after favor and love and joy that last forever. Are you? Is God's love your great treasure, or does the creature's love rival it? The grave proclaims that God's never-ending affection is the only sturdy, enduring source of satisfaction.

Second, a humble reckoning with our own death confronts us with the fleetingness of creaturely labor. The proud labor to erect monuments of accomplishment. Nebuchadnezzar's arrogance-filled question comes to mind: "Is not this great Babylon, that I have built for a royal dwelling by my mighty power and for the honor of my majesty?" (Dan. 4:30). Here is a man who built a glorious city in dependence on his own strength and for his own fame. But where is the great Babylon now? It is no greater than the decomposed corpse of Nebuchadnezzar in the ground. People's works die with them, and even if they outlive them, they will not last forever. Death "mercilessly mocks those who sleep through its lessons."[6] And that is why Moses pleads,

> Let Your work appear to Your servants,
> And Your glory to their children....
> And establish the work of our hands for us;
> Yes, establish the work of our hands. (Ps. 90:16–17)

The grave teaches us that all of our accomplishments are fleeting and meaningless unless God in His grace establishes them. Nothing we do will endure through time and eternity unless God sees fit to use it for His redemptive purposes. Grave-bound humility cries out to the Lord to cause enduring fruit to be born from our fleeting labors.

Think of the young mom whose day consists of an exhausting cycle of diaper changing, nose wiping, bottom spanking, and meal cooking. What is the point? Her toddler will not grow up remembering and thanking her for any of these things. Her husband won't express appreciation for half of what she does. And regardless, she

---

6. Daniel C. Fredericks, "Ecclesiastes," in *Ecclesiastes and the Song of Songs*, by Daniel C. Fredericks and Daniel J. Estes, Apollos Old Testament Commentary 16 (Downers Grove, Ill.: InterVarsity, 2010), 177.

changes one diaper only to be met with a stink five minutes later. It is all for nothing if God is not in the picture. But the humble mom desires her works to endure. As she goes about her days, she is ever praying, "O God, establish the work of my hands! Make these fleeting works to bear eternal fruit in the lives of my children, that they would see Your glorious power!" No proud mom prays like that. Only the humble lay hold of God to give enduring value to their endeavors for His glory.

While on his deathbed, John Owen summed up these humble lessons beautifully: "I am going to Him whom my soul hath loved, or rather who hath loved me with an everlasting love; which is the whole ground of all my consolation.... I am leaving the ship of the church in a storm, but whilst the great Pilot is in it the loss of a poor under-rower will be inconsiderable."[7] Owen knew unshakable comfort in the face of death because he had his sight affectionately set on his loving Creator and pilot, Jesus Christ. Christ would carry out the work, and Christ's love would never fail.

The Grave Is a School in Christ

Postfall humility, as we have seen, is not produced by a generic Godward self-perception but by a Christward self-perception. This Christward gaze is precisely what thoughts of our imminent death ought to bring about.

The gospel proclaims to us an eternal Creator who lovingly condescended to become a mortal creature. Without forfeiting His timeless deity, the Son of God became a dying man. He walked this earth with the constant and conscious awareness of a death sentence looming over His life. At the appointed time, His Father wrathfully cut Him down as the representative sin bearer. The command came on Calvary, "Return, O son of man!" and Jesus was swallowed up

---

7. As quoted in Sinclair B. Ferguson, introduction to *The Glory of Christ: His Office and Grace*, by John Owen (Fearn, Ross-shire, Scotland: Christian Focus, 2004), 20.

by mortality. His lifeless corpse was laid in the grave as He paid the infinite wages of sin to the last penny.

Consider that Psalm 90 is ultimately Jesus's prayer. He surely ·sang it and prayed it throughout His earthly life. And His loving Father answered these humble petitions. Jesus had basked under the love of His well-pleased Father for three decades. He didn't seek the favor of men but prized the heart of God above all. He labored in teaching and preaching and healing and training for three years, seeking the establishment of God's kingdom. But now this humble man is laid in the grave. All appears to be lost. Is death stronger than the Father's love? Is death the undoing of the Father's work? There is silence, darkness, grief. There are so many questions in the air.

But then on that epochal Sunday morning, Christ rose from the grave! The Father answered His Son's humble petitions, returning to His Son in favor, raising Him from the dead, satisfying His soul in the constancy of His steadfast love, and eternally establishing the work of His hands.

Here is a refuge for the humble believer in the face of death (Prov. 14:32). Here is what makes all the difference. Christ crucified and risen! Humility's preoccupation with the grave is founded on a more controlling preoccupation with Jesus in His risen splendor. When the grave tightens our grip and fixes our gaze on Christ, it makes us to be the most diligent laborers and sacrificial lovers imaginable.

- The risen Christ of the gospel assures us of God's everlasting love: "Who is he who condemns? It is Christ who died, and furthermore is also risen, who is even at the right hand of God, who also makes intercession for us. Who shall separate us from the love of Christ? Shall tribulation, or distress, or persecution, or famine, or nakedness, or peril, or sword?" (Rom. 8:34–35).

- The risen Christ of the gospel assures us of God's everlasting kingdom: The Father "raised Him from the dead and seated Him at His right hand in the heavenly places, far above all principality and power and might and dominion, and every name that is named, not only in this age but also in that which is to come" (Eph. 1:20–21).

- The risen Christ of the gospel assures us of God's everlasting establishment of us and our works: "Therefore, my beloved brethren, be steadfast, immovable, always abounding in the work of the Lord, knowing that your labor is not in vain in the Lord" (1 Cor. 15:58).

This is what gave John Owen such courage and strength in the face of the grave. As he lay dying, his final book was received for publication. It was a book on Christ's glory. Here was Owen's response to the soon publication of it: "I am glad to hear that that performance is put to the press; but…the long looked for day is come at last, in which I shall see that glory in another manner than I have ever done yet, or was capable of doing in this world!"[8] Owen had lived to behold Christ's beauty by faith, and now as he died, he eagerly anticipated beholding Christ's beauty by sight (2 Cor. 5:7).

For those who possess the downward disposition of a Christ-ward self-perception, death is the doorway to heavenly communion with their Beloved. In Christ, death is the doorway to life with the Lord as our dwelling place forevermore. Thomas Boston concurs:

Glory, glory, glory, blessing and praise to our Redeemer, our Saviour, our Mediator, by whose death, grim devouring death is made to do such a good office to those whom it might otherwise have hurried away in their wickedness, to utter and eternal destruction! A dying day is, in itself, a joyful day to the godly… the day in which the heirs of glory return from their travels, to their own country, and their Father's house, and enter into actual possession of the glorious inheritance.[9]

---

8. As quoted in Ferguson, introduction to *Glory of Christ*, 16.
9. Boston, *Human Nature in Its Fourfold State*, 357–58. Because of our remaining imperfection and unbelief, the day of death is not always a joyous day for the Christian. Boston goes on to address that (358–61).

Some Helps to Cultivating Humility through Death

In his excellent book *Remember Death*, Matthew McCullough encourages us to take up "death-awareness" as a "spiritual discipline."[10] Wilhelmus à Brakel calls us "to keep death continually in mind and to live continually with an impression of dying. This cannot be learned so readily, for we have a natural aversion for this and very quickly forget about death."[11]

How do we learn to number our days? What does it look like to discipline ourselves in the awareness that we are grave-bound mortals so that we might be growing ever lower in humility? Here are a few places to start.

First, see your own death in every death you encounter. Unless I am on a long road trip, I don't typically give thanks to God when I arrive safely at my destination. I just assume that I will make it. But I've been seeking this week to see my mortality in the death of my grandpa's best friend. Every time I arrive anywhere alive, it is only because God has preserved me from a myriad of potential deaths. And this has caused me to begin to acknowledge and praise Him, even if the drive is only five minutes. Don't merely seize on deaths that hit close to home but on every death, including those you encounter in the Bible or in the media. What was before a boring genealogy in Genesis 5 is intended to be a school in humility as over and again you read the refrain, "and he died…and he died… and he died."

Second, go for walks in cemeteries. On the day of my ordination exams, I sought a quiet place to pray and stumbled on a cemetery. As I prepared for the butcher block of sixty or so ordained men drilling me in theology, I found strange solace in reading the tombstones I walked past. Here was a far greater butcher block awaiting me than presbytery—the grave! But if Jesus had conquered that, then His grace would be sufficient in the lesser. There are so many lessons to learn from reading tombstones. One reality that struck me on that

---

10. McCullough, *Remember Death*, 21.
11. Brakel, *Christian's Reasonable Service*, 4:314.

particular day was how many of these people who had died were younger than I was. These were people with families and ambitions, but death took them early. Don't neglect the local cemetery.

Finally, see every new morning as a surprising gift from God. Death ought not to surprise us. Life should. How our hearts should be filled with gratitude when we wake up in the morning with hearts pumping, synapses firing, and lungs breathing. What astounding grace from God! Remind yourself of it every morning when your alarm clock goes off. And before you pick up your head from your pillow, freshly determine to live for God's glory for as many moments as He would keep you on this earth.

We are grave-bound mortals. Let us not pretend otherwise.

CHAPTER 14

Judgment-Bound Mortals

A half century ago, J. A. T. Robinson wrote, "We live…in a world without judgment, a world where at the last frontier post you simply go out—and nothing happens. It is like coming to the customs and finding there are none after all. And the suspicion that this is in fact the case spreads fast: for it is what we should all like to believe."[1] Before Robinson, the apostle Paul penned similar words about people who have suppressed the truth of God: "who, knowing the righteous judgment of God, that those who practice such things are deserving of death, not only do the same but also approve of those who practice them" (Rom. 1:32). People cannot enjoy their sin with judgment day looming over their heads. So they suppress what they know to be their future in order to enjoy the fleeting pleasures of the present. This is not a modern phenomenon; it is a universal phenomenon.[2] It is found whenever and wherever pride is found, for pride, being against God, is against His judgment.

---

1. J. A. T. Robinson, *On Being the Church in the World* (Harmondsworth, UK: Penguin, 1969), 165.

2. J. I. Packer states, "Retribution is the inescapable moral law of creation; God will see that each person sooner or later receives what he deserves—if not here, then hereafter. This is one of the basic facts of life. And, being made in God's image, we all know in our hearts that this is *right*. This is how it ought to be." *Knowing God*, 143.

The writer to the Hebrews states, "As it is appointed for men to die once, but after this the judgment, so Christ was offered once to bear the sins of many. To those who eagerly wait for Him He will appear a second time, apart from sin, for salvation" (9:27–28). Gravebound mortals are judgment-bound mortals. When the God-man comes again, He will come in judgment to consummate history as we know it. While the proud in Adam deny this reality, the humble in Christ await it with eagerness, even longing.

The Creator's Judgment Day Exaltation

The day of judgment will determine the eternal destiny of every image bearer of God. It is the doorway to our eternity. But it is not a day ultimately about the creature. "The outstanding purpose of the final judgment," writes Anthony Hoekema, "will be to display the sovereignty of God and the glory of God in the revelation of the final destiny of each person."[3] Judgment day is about the supreme manifestation of God in His holy majesty. Isaiah tells us that "the LORD alone shall be exalted in that day" (Isa. 2:11, 17). John explains that even earth and sky will flee from God's awesome presence (Rev. 20:11). God will be lifted up, forcing everyone and everything to reckon with His Godness. None will be able to escape their Creator on that day. Every person will come to possess a Godward self-perception.

Terrified without the Mediator

To say, however, that every person will possess a Godward self-perception is not to say that every person will possess God-fearing humility. All will see God with their physical eyes. All will be confronted with His fiery holiness and awesome supremacy. All will be

---

3. Anthony A. Hoekema, *The Bible and the Future* (Grand Rapids: Eerdmans, 1979), 254. Westminster Confession 33.2 likewise states, "The end of God's appointing this day is for the manifestation of the glory of his majesty, in the eternal salvation of the elect; and of his justice, in the damnation of the reprobate."

constrained to reckon with the truth of their Creator. But for the proud, this will not result in loving fear. Instead, it will give birth to carnal terror. The arrogant will cry out to the inanimate creation, "Fall on us and hide us from the face of Him who sits on the throne and from the wrath of the Lamb! For the great day of His wrath has come, and who is able to stand?" (Rev. 6:16–17). This is not the worship-producing, consecration-provoking, love-besotted fear that bedecks the souls of the humble; this is the petrified terror of proud sinners before their holy Creator with nowhere to run or hide. This is a Godward self-perception without Christ, the Mediator.

Try to fathom for a moment what it would be like to stand before God without the Mediator. All your life, you lived to suppress the truth of God and His law. But now God is forcing the full weight of His righteous glory on you. You are seeing Him in His infinite holiness. You are seeing yourself in your deplorable, God-hating depravity. The guilty conscience that you learned to silence from your youth is now louder than a blood-curdling scream or a blaring siren. The God whose worship you trifled with, whose word you despised, and whose world you abused is now standing before you—and there is no escaping His wrath. No second chances. No offer of mercy. No purgatory. God in His terrifying justice is all that is left.

Does such a thought cause you to tremble? I'm convicted as I write that question. "Oh, how dreadfully they all will wail and cry and lament!" exclaims Theodorus VanderGroe. "How the air will then be filled with the distressful groaning and weeping of all the damned! How the earth will then be saturated by their cold sweat and salty tears!"[4] For sinners like us to meet God without the Mediator is more terrifying than meeting ten thousand atomic bombs. And there will be no bomb shelter to run to for cover.

---

4. Theodorus VanderGroe, *The Christian's Only Comfort in Life and Death: An Exposition of the Heidelberg Catechism*, trans. Bartel Elshout, ed. Joel R. Beeke (Grand Rapids: Reformation Heritage Books, 2016), 1:415.

John envisions the proud hiding "in the caves and in the rocks of the mountains" (Rev. 6:15). Isaiah, with a hint of sarcasm, commands God's unrepentant people,

Enter into the rock, and hide in the dust,
From the terror of the LORD
And the glory of His majesty. (Isa. 2:10)

They had exalted the creation above the Creator, and so the creation is the only place they have to turn. But on that day, "the idols He shall utterly abolish" (v. 18). The creation they idolized will be of no help to them.

- They won't be able to hide behind bank accounts, academic degrees, or earthly toys and treasures. When face-to-face with God, what are all humanity's vain pursuits?
- They won't be able to draw the slightest comfort from the human applause and approval they once lived for. When face-to-face with God, what is humanity's opinion?
- They won't be able to find the least pleasure in the food, drink, sex, and entertainment they once found satisfaction in. When face-to-face with God, what could possibly be enjoyed?

In Isaiah's vision, it is not God smashing idols on judgment day. The proud are the ones doing it. They are forced to face the miserable reality that nothing in the created order can save them from their Creator.

In that day a man will cast away his idols of silver
And his idols of gold,
Which they made, each for himself to worship,
To the moles and bats. (Isa. 2:20)

Think of all your earthly possessions, accomplishments, and relationships—none of it will prove of any use on this day. Like Adam's fig leaves, nothing in creation can shield the proud from the wrath of God.

Delighted with the Mediator

The same event that engulfs the proud with terror absorbs the humble in happy delight. What makes the difference? Christ! In life, the humble had trusted in Him. They recognized their corruption in Adam and had cast themselves entirely on Jesus. By God's grace, they came to possess the downward disposition of a Christward self-perception.

The "day of wrath and revelation of the righteous judgment of God" (Rom. 2:5) will be a joy to them because Christ already suffered their wrath and swallowed it up. The cross was Christ's "day of wrath," leaving not a drop left in the cup of God's holy anger for them to drink. There will be no need to hide under rocks and mountains, for they are hidden in the righteous refuge of Christ. They will not be filled with the agonizing realization that no creaturely idol can deliver them, for Christ is their life and joy.

More than this, the Mediator in whom the humble trust will Himself be the Judge, for the Father "has appointed a day on which He will judge the world in righteousness by the Man whom He has ordained. He has given assurance of this to all by raising Him from the dead" (Acts 17:31). The judgment seat of God (Rom. 14:10 ESV) is nothing less than the judgment seat of Christ (2 Cor. 5:10). On that day, the glory of God will be exalted in and through the incarnate Son. Judgment day is Christ's "final exaltation and highest triumph."[5] Herein He forever vanquishes His enemies and vindicates His friends. Herein His work is consummated. If such a thought doesn't delight your heart, you have reason to question your humility!

While the Christless proud will be filled with a fear that drives them from God on this final day, the Christward humble will be filled with a fear that drives them toward God. The glorious appearing of their Savior will be the perfecting of their Godward self-perception, ushering them into "an unprecedented joyful fear of the Redeemer."[6]

---

5. Hoekema, *Bible and the Future*, 256.
6. Reeves, *Rejoice and Tremble*, 157.

The Creature's Judgment Day Humiliation

The Creator's exaltation necessarily leads to the creature's humiliation. The creature cannot encounter the Creator without being cut down to size.

As a kid you may have suffered at the hands of a playground bully. He pushed you off your swing. He flung mud in your face. He made fun of your hairstyle. Third-grade Billy thought he was big stuff as he berated and walloped you. But imagine that one day, as he is showering you with degrading remarks, he perceives a large shadow looming over him. He turns around to find none other than your dad, who has come to pick you up from school. What happens to "big" Billy in that moment? He suddenly understands he is not as tall and strong as he imagined himself to be. Your dad doesn't even say a word. He doesn't even lift a finger. He just shows up, and Billy is brought low.

That is what will happen on judgment day. Christ won't have to wrestle people to the dirt. He won't have to resort to persuasive words to convince them to get low. He will simply show up, and the weight of His majesty will force all else to the dust.

An Unhumble Humiliation

Not all humiliation leads to humility, and that will certainly be the case on the last day. Isaiah says of this day,

> The lofty looks of man shall be humbled,
> The haughtiness of men shall be bowed down,
> And the LORD alone shall be exalted in that day. (Isa. 2:11)

What kind of humbling is this? Is Isaiah foretelling a day of grace wherein God so reveals His majesty that people are genuinely humbled and willingly bow and worship Him? No, this is not a willful humbling brought about by divine grace. This is a forced humbling brought about by terrifying wrath. This is third-grade Billy cowering before your dad not as an expression of loving respect, but as an expression of self-preserving contempt. The prophet expands on this,

using the word "against" ten times in verses 12–16 (ESV) to empha-
size the wrath of God, which will forcefully drive people downward:

> For the LORD of hosts has a day
>   against all that is proud and lofty,
>   against all that is lifted up—and it shall be brought low;
> against all the cedars of Lebanon,
>   lofty and lifted up;
>   and against all the oaks of Bashan;
> against all the lofty mountains,
>   and against all the uplifted hills;
> against every high tower,
>   and against every fortified wall;
> against all the ships of Tarshish,
>   and against all the beautiful craft.

The repetition is intended to wake us up to the terrifying nature of
this future reality. The humbling brought about here is not humility;
it is actually a final hardening in pride as creatures attempt by whatever means possible to escape the Creator, who is against them.
Prideful man wants to be man-in-himself. Prideful woman wants to
be a law unto herself. But judgment day forces all image bearers to
come to terms with their moral accountability to their Maker.

Judgment entails some standard by which to judge. The standard by which Christ will judge the proud is His revelation in both
nature and the Scriptures.

The proud live in a world that is everywhere revealing the glory
of God (Rom. 1:18–20). As the image of God, they have His law written on their hearts (2:14–15). Every one of their thoughts, desires,
intentions, words, and actions will be judged according to this universal revelation of God and His moral will. God has so revealed
Himself in the natural order that the proud "are without excuse" for
their rejection of Him (1:20). The Greek literally reads that they "are
without *an apologetic*." Sinful people will not have a defense attor-
ney on judgment day. There won't be a single shred of evidence to
present in their favor. That is true simply by virtue of being the image
of God in a world created and governed by God.

People's inexcusability is only heightened for those who encounter God's revelation in the Scriptures, for it is in the Bible that God reveals Christ and His salvation. Jesus had preached and performed miracles in Capernaum, but despite the revelation of His grace and power, the city remained hardened in pride, leading to His prophetic warning, "You, Capernaum, who are exalted to heaven, will be brought down to Hades; for if the mighty works which were done in you had been done in Sodom, it would have remained until this day. But I say to you that it shall be more tolerable for the land of Sodom in the day of judgment than for you" (Matt. 11:23–24). Jesus pointed them to Sodom—that sin-sick, pride-infected city consumed in the fire of God's wrath—and urged, "Look at Sodom. All they had was God's revelation in nature. They didn't have the Christ. But you have Me, and you have rejected Me! They didn't have the Bible. But you have God's word, and you have disbelieved it! God has given you much, and you have squandered it in your arrogance. Therefore, judgment day will be more terrible for you than for any Sodomite unless you humble yourself in repentance now!" How dreadful this day will be for those who had Christ held out to them in life but rejected His offer of grace. How absolutely petrifying to stand before the Lord, whom they mocked and disdained all their days.

The God of gospel grace will now be forever against the proud in wrath. On this day, "to those who are self-seeking and do not obey the truth, but obey unrighteousness," there will be nothing but "indignation and wrath" (Rom. 2:8). Those who bow the knee to the self now ("those who are self-seeking") will be forced to bow the knee to Christ then. Those who live in God-suppressing sin now ("those who…do not obey the truth, but obey unrighteousness") will be forced to acknowledge their creaturely accountability and culpability then. They will be humbled by wrath while never becoming genuinely humble. They will possess a Godward self-perception while never becoming loving God fearers. That, as we will see in the next chapter, is hell. That is the ultimate curse. That is the Hades to which the haughty will be forced down.

A Humble Humiliation

But what about the humble? Will they too be brought low on judgment day? The Scriptures emphatically deny that the humble will be cut down by a God who is against them in terrifying wrath. But there is still a humiliation that will take place for the humble. We sometimes forget that God will judge all peoples "according to their works" (Rev. 20:12–13). Humble believers will give an account to Christ. Every secret will be laid bare, every deed set forth. "For we must all appear before the judgment seat of Christ, that each one may receive the things done in the body, according to what he has done, whether good or bad" (2 Cor. 5:10). On the final day, the lowly in spirit will own their creatureliness in a more pervasive way than they ever did while in the mortal body. For the first time, they will perfectly grasp the absolute authority of their fatherly Creator over them as their deeds are judged.

But aren't the humble saved by faith apart from works? Isn't it Christ's work that leads to our acquittal before God? On the surface it appears that a judgment of the humble according to works would promote self-sufficient pride, not humility. We may be tempted to think that a fixation on works would cause us to lose our Christward gaze. But it causes nothing of the sort!

The faith by which the humble are saved is a faith that works by love (Gal. 5:6), and love fulfills the law (Rom. 13:8). This is why James tells us that "faith by itself, if it does not have works, is dead" (James 2:17). The believer's works are not the ground of God declaring him or her righteous on judgment day. Christ's work is. But the faith that lays hold of Christ is a faith that bears the fruit of God-fearing, people-loving obedience. Richard Gaffin explains that for believers, "good works will not be the ground or basis of their acquittal. Nor are they (co-) instrumental, a coordinate instrument for appropriating divine approbation as they supplement faith. Rather, they are the essential and manifest criterion of that faith."[7] There is

---

7. Richard B. Gaffin Jr., *By Faith, Not by Sight: Paul and the Order of Salvation*, 2nd ed. (Phillipsburg, N.J.: P&R, 2013), 112.

no smuggling in of an arrogant works-righteousness principle here. Faith eyes Christ alone, but people cannot be savingly attached to Christ without their motivations, thoughts, words, and actions being radically transformed.

The good works of the humble revealed on judgment day are Christ's work. Believers are "created *in Christ Jesus* for good works" (Eph. 2:10). They work out their salvation only because Christ works in them "both to will and to do for His good pleasure" (Phil. 2:12–13). Apart from Him they can bear no good fruit (John 15:5). Our good works in Christ will serve to magnify His gracious power, not our native self-sufficiency. This is especially so given that even the best works of the humble are shot through with pride. God is pleased with the imperfect holiness of the humble because their good works are tethered to the perfectly humble Christ. Calvin writes:

> After forgiveness of sins is set forth, the good works that now follow are appraised otherwise than on their own merit. For everything imperfect in them is covered by Christ's perfection, every blemish or spot is cleansed away by his purity in order not to be brought into question at the divine judgment. Therefore, after the guilt of all transgressions that hinder man from bringing forth anything pleasing to God has been blotted out, and after the fault of imperfection, which habitually defiles even good works, is buried, the good works done by believers are accounted righteous.[8]

Rather than provoking the humble to depend on themselves and their own righteousness, their judgment according to works will highlight in glorified finality the saving sufficiency of Christ and their entire dependence on Him. Every sin laid bare will serve to magnify Christ's sin-defeating sacrifice. Every good yet imperfect work will serve to magnify Christ's moral flawlessness. Standing before the God-man as Judge, the humble will experience the perfection of a Christward self-perception and thus of humility's downward disposition. Because of their elder Brother, they will now come into full

---

8. Calvin, *Institutes*, 3.17.8.

possession of all the rights and privileges of God's children. They will be openly and publicly vindicated. Their sonship will be revealed for all creation to see, and they will be ushered into their Father's heavenly house and eternal embrace.

Longing for Judgment Day

Do you see why Christ's coming to judge the world in righteousness is the "blessed hope" of the humble (Titus 2:13)? Think about those two words—"blessed hope." *Hope* refers not to wishful thinking, but to confident expectation. It is a forward-looking virtue founded on the sure testimony of God. *Blessed* describes something that brings soul-satisfying, joy-filled delight. That is what judgment day is to lowly believers in Jesus. It is a day they look forward to with confident longing because they will then be ushered into ultimate blessedness. Then, they will be forever done with pride. Then, they will perfectly acknowledge their need of Christ. Then, they will perfectly know the love of Christ. Nothing do they aspire after more than to hear their Lord say, "Well done, good and faithful servant.... Enter into the joy of your lord" (Matt. 25:23). Nothing gets them out of bed in the morning quite like the thought of Christ's welcoming words: "Come, you blessed of My Father, inherit the kingdom prepared for you from the foundation of the world" (v. 34). Judgment day is no speculative theory or impractical truth. It drives believers in every place and at all times to live from Christ, through Christ, and to Christ. The day that will serve to perfect their humility produces humility in them now as they live in the eager expectation of Christ's imminent return.

CHAPTER 15

Eternity-Bound Mortals

Christianity is a future-oriented religion ever calling us to lift our eyes to what is to come. But how many of us actually do? We fixate much on the past and on the present. We draft detailed plans for and dream about our uncertain future in this world. But how much of our attention is devoted to meditating on the certain realities of the grave, the judgment, and the eternal state? Eschatology is often disparaged as an abstract discipline for PhD intellectuals. But God wills for it to be a practical discipline for humble Christians. He wills for these future certainties to radically change how we face our present uncertainties.

The Bible calls this *hope*. We use the word frequently, saying things like, "I hope the preacher isn't longwinded this morning," or "I hope she lands the job." *Hope* in modern terms refers to a desire for a future outcome that is presently undetermined. It is mere wishful thinking. But *hope* in biblical terms refers to a confident expectation in God and His promises. It is rock-solid, forward-looking certainty rooted in the unchanging God and His perfect word.

Humility is not only intimately related to Godward fear and humanward love but also to futureward hope. The lower we grow, the more hopeful we become. The proud might have wishful thinking regarding their eternity, but they are strangers to the unshakable security of biblical hope. Pride is always asking the question, Did God really say? Such revelation-rejecting, God-disrespecting arrogance leaves people with nothing but the uncertain postulations of the autonomous self. Only the humble, who tremble at God's word, can have rock-solid confidence as they look to the future. Only they can eye the days to come with joyous expectation and sober fear.

As we have seen with regard to death and the judgment, the more the humble hope, the humbler they become. For by God's good design, these future certainties promote the downward disposition of a Christward self-perception. We turn in this last chapter to the final state of both the proud and the humble. Christian hope is not ultimately fixated on death or the judgment, but on the eternal. All of us are eternity-bound mortals swiftly moving toward our final and forever destination. And humility, or the lack thereof, is the great determiner of our destiny.

Pride's Final Destination

On judgment day Christ, with inescapable authority, will command the arrogant, "Depart from Me, you cursed, into the everlasting fire prepared for the devil and his angels" (Matt. 25:41). What woeful words! They set before us how heinous pride truly is. It warrants consummate curse and eternal fire. Hell exists because of Satan's pride. It is Satan's final destination, and it is the final destination of all his spiritual children who unrepentantly seek to usurp their Creator's authority (Rev. 20:10, 15).

Those who have little appetite for the doctrine of hell will have little appetite for the preaching of Christ. It is no exaggeration to label our Lord a hellfire preacher. He was not afraid to call people to tremble before the Creator, "who is able to destroy both soul and body in hell" (Matt. 10:28). He didn't shrink back from warning of the hell that awaits those who fail to humbly make war on their sin (5:27–30). To depart into hell, according to Jesus, was not to cease to exist (i.e., annihilationism), but to continue to exist in a place of "everlasting fire" and "everlasting punishment" (25:41, 46). Throughout His ministry, Jesus warned of this, but nowhere did He provide us with a clearer glimpse into the pit than in the parable of the rich man and Lazarus (Luke 16:19–31). Parable is a powerful way to communicate truth, and Jesus utilized it to vividly explain the final destiny of the proud.

In His parable we are introduced to two very different men. The one is rich; the other is poor. The one lives in a gated home; the other is homeless. The one is dressed in royalty; the other is adorned by rags. The one is feasting; the other is starving. The one is healthy; the other is covered in sores. But these are mere superficial differences, pointing us to the real difference—the rich man is proud; the poor man is humble. The rich man worships the god of material prosperity (i.e., the creation); the poor man worships the God of Abraham (i.e., the Creator). And so at death, in verse 22 humble Lazarus is "carried by the angels to Abraham's bosom" (a clear reference to heaven), while the prideful rich man in verse 23 descends into "Hades" (a clear reference to hell).

The Agony of Hell

Jesus describes the rich man's condition in hell with three words: "being in torments" (Luke 16:23). A more literal translation would read: "*in possession* of torments." On earth this man possessed every pleasure imaginable, but now his only possession is pain. In fact, *pain* is far too weak a word. This is severe, agonizing, torturous pain consuming both body and soul. The rich man describes his experience this way: "I am in anguish in this flame" (v. 24 ESV).

What exactly makes hell so agonizing? It is not the presence of the devil, sporting red spandex and poking people with a pitchfork. Hell is agonizing precisely because God is there in all of His blazing holiness. God's wrath is being unleashed on this man, and he has absolutely nowhere to hide.

The proud in hell are left in a condition of unrestrained pride with every possible avenue of satisfying their idolatrous desires removed. They worshiped their belly while on earth, and now they crave for a rich feast but find not a crumb to consume. They worshiped sex while on earth, and now they lust with unrestrained intensity but find no means of satisfying their sexual desires. All of their gods are gone. Only the true God remains. That is pride's worst nightmare.

The Duration of Hell

Jesus's parable presents us with a man experiencing wave upon wave of unmitigated divine wrath with no end in sight. His cry for deliverance is met with the matter-of-fact statement from the heaven-dwelling Abraham: "Between us and you there is a great gulf fixed, so that those who want to pass from here to you cannot, nor can those from there pass to us" (Luke 16:26). There is no way out of hell. It is a dead-end, forever destination.

God is infinite in holiness, and our defiance of Him incurs an infinite debt that finite creatures like us can never pay—hence, a punishment of infinite duration. Some people tragically suffer from chronic physical pain for decades, but hell entails the most agonizing pain possible, and everlastingly so. Edward Payson writes, "The fire of his anger must burn forever. It is a fire, which cannot be quenched, unless God should change or cease to exist. It is this, which constitutes the most terrible ingredient of that cup, which impenitent sinners must drink."[1] If the torment of hell were anything less than eternal, the proud sinner could draw comfort from the prospect of relief. But such is not the case. Think of the agony produced by the conscious realization of the eternality of agony. The proud residents of hell, warns Thomas Goodwin, "shall not outlive that misery… having for ever to do with him who is the living God."[2]

The rich man lived for this world. He worshiped power, possessions, popularity, and pleasure. Be sure of it—these things provided him with temporary satisfaction. Sin satisfies. Pride most definitely brings joy, but only temporarily and superficially. Note Abraham's response to this rich man as he cries out for relief: "Son, remember

---

1. Edward Payson, *The Complete Works of Edward Payson* (Harrisonburg, Va.: Sprinkle Publications, 1988), 2:327.
2. Thomas Goodwin, *Two Discourses* (London: J. D. for Jonathan Robinson, 1693), 195.

that in your lifetime you received your good things…but now…
you are tormented" (Luke 16:25). The Creator had offered the rich
man eternal joy in Himself, but he pridefully exchanged it for temporary joy in the creation. And Abraham is saying, "You got what
you wanted. You worshiped temporary things; you got temporary
joy. But now there is everlasting woe to be endured for your arrogant
idolatry." Thomas Boston remarks, "The pleasures of sin are bought
too dear, at the rate of everlasting burnings."[3] Don't just breeze over
that. Think about it. Consider the folly of pride—temporary pleasures purchased at the price of eternal torment. Hell shows us just
how insane our prideful hearts are.

The Evangelism of Hell

If my aspiration in life was to become a best-selling author, I would
fare much better by writing a personal account of my descent into
hell than by writing a practical theology of humility.[4] Humility is not
a recipe for making the *New York Times* best-seller list, but temporarily being transported to the afterlife only to return to publish your
experience sells big! The popularity of such accounts today reveals
just how proud we are, for it is the precise evangelistic strategy of the
rich man in hell. When he comes to recognize that hell has no exit,
he desperately pleads with Abraham, "I beg you therefore, father, that
you would send [Lazarus] to my father's house, for I have five brothers, that he may testify to them, lest they also come to this place of
torment" (Luke 16:27).

But humble Abraham is not persuaded in the least. "They have
Moses and the prophets," he replies, "let them hear them" (Luke 16:29).
To which this proud, agonizing man responds, "No, father Abraham;
but if one goes to them from the dead, they will repent" (v. 30).

---

3. Boston, *Human Nature in Its Fourfold State*, 491.
4. The phrase "evangelism of hell" is taken from Ian Macleod, "They Have
Moses and the Prophets" (sermon, Free Reformed Church, Grand Rapids,
Michigan, May 8, 2016), https://www.sermonaudio.com/sermoninfo.asp?SID
=54161825403.

It is important to recognize that the rich man is a Jew. That is clear from the context, as well as from his repeated address of Abraham as father. Here is what this proud, unbelieving Jew is saying: "Abraham, you clearly don't understand. The Bible did nothing for me. I grew up being taught from it. I heard it every Sabbath. I could quote large portions of it. And here I am in this agonizing torment." He is emphatically arguing that something more is needed than the Christ of Scripture.

Maybe the Bible works for some people. Maybe preaching works in some cultures—but not here and now. You know what would really convince people in this day, according to some?

- If Charles Darwin arose, renouncing the folly of atheism and warning of the wrath to come.
- If Hugh Hefner arose, renouncing the folly of eroticism and warning of the wrath to come.
- If Michael Jackson arose, renouncing the folly of materialism and warning of the wrath to come.

The Bible—it is good and fine, but it is not sufficient. That is pride's mantra. It is what led to humanity's original demise. Adam and Eve didn't prize God's authoritative word. They played God, standing in judgment over His absolutely authoritative and sufficient revelation. This is our great problem. This is the great reason why hell exists. And this is why the parable concludes with the sobering words of Abraham left ringing in our ears: "If they do not hear Moses and the prophets, neither will they be persuaded though one rise from the dead" (Luke 16:31).

You can avoid eternal fire by one road alone—humble faith in the Christ of the Scriptures. But this is the precise road the feet of the proud never dare to tread. They refuse to bow to Christ's word because they refuse to bow to Christ. They don't mind religion as long as they can continue to swear ultimate allegiance to the supreme self. Thus, the proud, dying in arrogant unbelief, abide forever under the perpetual wrath of their Creator.

Hellfire Humility
Do you see now why pride is your greatest enemy? Left unmortified, it will lead to your eternal undoing. It is so easy to have notions of hell in our heads but not in our hearts. How we need the Spirit of God to emblazon these horrifying realities on us! The hell reserved for the proud ought to profoundly deepen our humility. Gaze into the pit and see your Creator's uncompromising holiness. He is not to be trifled with. Gaze into the pit and see how heinous your creaturely defiance is and how helpless you are to deliver yourself from it. Eternal torment is what you deserve. What a controlling sense of our creaturely corruption hell ought to work in us, and how it ought to cause us to cast ourselves in humble trust on Christ! For "Christ himself has felt the pains of hell for you," writes Thomas Watson. "The Lamb of God being roasted in the fire of God's wrath, by this burnt-offering the Lord is now appeased toward His people."[5] The reality of hell driven home to the heart of the believer cannot fail to produce the downward disposition of a Christward self-perception.

Humility's Final Destination
Abraham's words to the rich man make plain that the eternal destiny of all people depends on their response to the Bible. The proud rejection of God's revelation ends in hell precisely because it is a rejection of the revelation of Jesus Christ, who alone can save. But the humble, bowing before and embracing the Mediator, have a markedly different end. They are represented, foreloved, and adopted believers, trusting solely in the crucified and risen God-man. Like humble Lazarus, they worship the God of Abraham and are heirs of His eternal household.

The Bible closes with the premier hope of the humble as John records his vision of "a new heaven and a new earth" (Rev. 21:1; cf. Isa. 65:17). This Spirit-transformed world is a garden-temple

5. Thomas Watson, *The Christian on the Mount: A Treatise on Meditation*, ed. Don Kistler (Orlando, Fla.: Northampton Press, 2009), 57.

similar to Eden, only remarkably better, for this garden has no serpent. Satan, along with his angelic and human followers, has been cast into hell. More than that, this garden has no possibility of loss. The dwellers, beholding Christ, have been perfectly and irreversibly transformed into His image. This is a prideless world of unbounded blessedness. This is the eternal life that the first Adam would have attained had he rejected the serpent's deceit.

A World of Perfect Adoration

The inhabitants of the world to come enjoy the soul-nourishing waters of the river of life and the sweetly satisfying fruit of the tree of life (Rev. 22:1–2). The final destination of the humble is a place of undiluted life, and the life is God Himself. As Jesus made plain during His earthly ministry, eternal life is nothing other than reconciled, loving communion with the Father through the Son (John 17:3). Knowing God, delighting in God, loving God, living with God—this is eternal life. This is the life of the new earth.

The central feature in John's vision is "the throne of God and of the Lamb" (Rev. 22:3). God in Christ is reigning as the uncontested Lord. None are vying for the throne. None are envious of His exalted position.

Every inhabitant is simply adoring Him (Rev. 22:3). John explains, "They shall see His face, and His name shall be on their foreheads" (v. 4). The people in this garden-temple no longer see God by faith or through the glass of the Scriptures. They are beholding God with glorified human eyes—physical eyeballs that have been transformed by the Spirit, enabling them to fixate on God's blinding glory without being consumed. This is nothing less than a glorified Godward gaze. But it is more than that. The inhabitants of the new earth enjoy a perfect and perpetual Christward gaze. For the glory of God that pervades their vision ever shines through the "lamp" of the Lamb (Rev. 21:23 ESV).

The perfection of a Christward self-perception entails the perfection of humility's downward disposition. Thus, the inhabitants of the new earth are doing what God's image was originally created to do. They are enjoying and glorifying Him forever. Jonathan Edwards proclaims, "The glorious excellencies and beauty of God will be what will forever entertain the minds of the saints, and the love of God will be their everlasting feast."[6] Worship is the perpetual vocation of this humble people. As the high priest under the old covenant had God's name on his forehead, so too do the inhabitants of this land (Rev. 22:4). They are priests. As the holy of holies was a perfect cube, so too is this garden-city (21:15–17). They are dwelling forevermore in God's house.

Such a vision is utterly repulsive to the proud. Pride seeks nothing more than to avoid the face of God. But here we find a people of perfect humility, relishing in the beauty of God through the Mediator. Here is perfect dependence on God, perfect submission to Him, and perfect delight in Him. Here is the creature rightly relating to the Creator, and never without a sense of indebtedness to the Lamb. Here is perfect humility forever!

Does the sight cause your soul to groan with longing? Does your heart yearn for nothing more than to be ever done with the God-belittling folly of pride? The day is fast approaching for all who possess such Spirit-wrought longings.

A World of Perfect Exaltation

The humble of this land don't worship before God only as glorified priests, but they also reign with Him as glorified kings. That is how John's vision ends: "And they shall reign forever and ever" (Rev. 22:5).

But isn't the Lord alone exalted and every creature brought low? Yes, God is the sole King of this land. There are no rival thrones to His. But here the humble are brought to share in the exalted reign of God Himself.

Think back to the first time Dad let you drive the car. You were four or five years old. Your legs weren't long enough to reach the gas

6. Jonathan Edwards, "God Glorified in Man's Dependence," in *Sermons and Discourses, 1730–1733*, ed. Mark Valeri (New Haven, Conn.: Yale University Press, 1999), 208.

pedal. Your arms weren't strong enough to turn the steering wheel. But Dad sat you on his lap in the driver's seat as the two of you drove around the neighborhood. When you arrived home, you ran into the house and exclaimed, "Mom, I drove the car!" You were not lying. After all, you were in the driver's seat. Your hand was on the wheel. But Mom knew, of course, that it was Dad driving the car the whole time.

That is what is happening in the new earth. God is putting His humble children on His lap as He sits enthroned over all. The dominion that Adam was called to exercise is realized. God alone is the uppercase King, but His children, united to their elder Brother, reign with Him forever as lowercase kings. They share in His cosmic victory as His kingdom encompasses the whole earth.

The eternal reign of the humble is what we should expect, for it has been God's purpose and promise all along. It is the consummation of the grace promised to the lowly (Prov. 3:34). It is the final realization of Christ's own words: "Whoever exalts himself will be humbled, and he who humbles himself will be exalted" (Luke 14:11). The perfectly humble are being lifted up to the throne of God itself. This profound lowliness is being everlastingly wed to a profound height. God's children are following in the steps of His once-humiliated and now-exalted Son.

The Hope of the Humble

Geerhardus Vos once said, "The air of the world to come is the vital atmosphere which [the Christian] delights to breathe and outside of which he feels depressed and languid."[7] When astronauts go into outer space, they take the earth's air with them. They cannot live without breathing the atmosphere of their home planet. Vos is saying that the Christian, being in a foreign place, must breathe the air of his true home. The oxygen of the new earth is what fills his spiritual lungs. It is what enables him to press on in this wilderness. It is what gives

---

7. Geerhardus Vos, "A Sermon on 1 Peter 1:3–5," https://www.kerux.com/doc/0102A1.asp.

energy and life to his devotion. The humble live on "the vital atmosphere" of the new earth.

Heaven's air is not only in their spiritual lungs, but heaven's glory pervades their spiritual eyes. As I wrote this chapter, two words from one of my favorite hymns were impressed on my heart in a fresh way—"bright hope." These words are from the final stanza of Thomas O. Chisholm's "Great Is Thy Faithfulness":

Pardon for sin and a peace that endureth,
Thine own dear presence to cheer and to guide,
Strength for today and bright hope for tomorrow;
Blessings all mine, with ten thousand beside.[8]

I have sung those words countless times, but I'm not sure I have ever considered them seriously. Bright hope. How brilliantly bright is the hope of the humble in Jesus Christ! As an eternity-bound mortal, is the gaze of your soul fixed on it?

If you are trusting in Christ alone for salvation, you will one day soon come to share in God's loving rule as you worshipfully bask in His loving presence forevermore, eternally loved children everlastingly enjoying their Father's affectionate presence through their elder Brother. This, writes B. B. Warfield, is "the consummated purpose of the immeasurable love of God."[9] This is adoption raised in glorified finality. This is not wishful thinking or groundless optimism. This is the hope of the humble, compelling them to cry here below, "Come, Lord Jesus! Come quickly!" (see Rev. 22:20).

---

8. Thomas O. Chisholm, "Great Is Thy Faithfulness," in the public domain.
9. B. B. Warfield, *The Saviour of the World* (Edinburgh: Banner of Truth, 1991), 130.

Conclusion

At many points throughout the writing journey, I dreamed of arriving at the conclusion. Some days I questioned whether I would ever reach it. But here we are, and honestly, it is not how I imagined it would be.

I anticipated breathing a huge sigh of relief and feeling an overwhelming sense of accomplishment. I envisioned blowing a kazoo, throwing confetti in the air, and performing a victory dance. But my imagination was void of humble realism.

Don't misunderstand me. Humility is not against kazoos and confetti. But my gratitude to God in these moments is mixed with a sorrow I didn't anticipate. I find a restless ache and sober uneasiness within.

As I look at my own heart, I see a man who knows a lot about humility. As I look at my congregation, I see a church well stocked with truths about humility (having sat through a twenty-plus-message sermon series on the theme). But the disquieting question is, Are we any humbler for having come to grasp this virtue more clearly? Is humility an intimate friend radically changing us at the core of our beings? Have we actually grown downward? And are we continuing to grow lower still?

The dangerous thing about reading (and writing) a book on humility is that you reach the end thinking you've obtained it. But the mere reading of this book will not make you humble. In fact, it could do just the opposite. Knowing about a Christward self-perception will make you proud if that knowledge falls short of genuinely orienting your affections toward Christ. And that is the reason for my restlessness and uneasiness in these moments.

I still find it difficult to make the psalmist's words my own: "LORD, my heart is not haughty" (Ps. 131:1). I desire to say this in truth, and there is a sense in which, by God's grace, I can. But there is another sense in which I feel insincere having David's words on my lips. My heart is so tirelessly prone to exalted thoughts of the self. Pride distorts my every move. The book may be written, and the book may be read, but the pursuit of humility has only just begun—and hence the inward restlessness with reference to myself and the church.

How we need the Spirit to work mightily within us and revive us! Revival, after all, is nothing less than the Spirit's work of exalting Christ in the hearts of His people. Revival is the extraordinary blessing of Christ's Spirit on the ordinary means of grace, leading God's children to see and savor the soul-satisfying beauty of Jesus. The Spirit alone can grow us upward in loving fear of Christ so that we grow downward in humility.

Let us set our faces to seek the Spirit for this. Let us pray and pray and pray! As you reach the final page of this book, plead with God to expose the layers of hidden pride within your heart. Pray that He would grow you downward in humility, upward in fear, and outward in love. Ask Him to give you strength to comprehend in the depths of your soul what it is to be His eternally loved child, justified and sanctified in Christ Jesus, to His praise and glory. Set your face to seek Him for these things daily. Octavius Winslow writes, "The prayer of a child of God should unceasingly be, that the Lord would keep him *from himself*; that the posture of his mind might be low at the feet of Jesus, each moment learning of, and living to him."[1] Oh to live in such a state of perpetual, dependent, adoring lowliness before our Lord! Do you long for it? Those who do seek after it earnestly.

---

1. Winslow, *Personal Declension and Revival of Religion*, 156.

Do not ask for yourself alone but for your family and your church to become increasingly captivated by the glory and goodness of God in Jesus Christ. Pray for the unbelievers in your life, that God would wake them up from their Christ-hating arrogance and cause them to know the sweetness and saving power of His love. Pray for a revival of creaturely lowliness around the globe.

The great need of the church in every age is Christ-exalting humility. To the degree the church possesses this, it will be alive and advancing with vigor. To the degree the church lacks this virtue, it will be lethargic and on its way to the grave.

May Christ see fit to grow His people ever downward in this blessed virtue to His glory, honor, and praise. And may my feeble attempt in these pages to exalt the Savior and to humble the sinner be one means the Spirit wields toward that end. *Soli Deo gloria.*